# Salt-Free Cooking
## with Herbs and Spices

# Salt-Free Cooking with Herbs and Spices

## June Roth

Foreword by
S. K. Fineberg, M.D., F.A.C.P.

Contemporary Books, Inc.
Chicago

Published by Contemporary Books, Inc.
180 North Michigan Avenue, Chicago, Illinois 60601
Manufactured in the United States of America
Library of Congress Catalog Card Number: 77-81178
International Standard Book Number: 0-8092-8251-8 (cloth)
0-8092-7722-0 (paper)

Published simultaneously in Canada by
Beaverbooks, Ltd.
150 Lesmill Road
Don Mills, Ontario M3B 2T5
Canada

To my dear friend Roslyn,
whose memory remains an inspiration
to all who knew and loved her.

# Contents

# Foreword

The most important reason for reducing or nearly eliminating common salt (sodium chloride) and other sodium-containing substances from the diet is to control hypertension, commonly called high blood pressure. If salt intake is reduced early in the treatment of hypertension, the chances are greatly improved that the slow development of serious consequences will be prevented. In simple terms, these complications are the result of a hastening of the aging process in the arteries of vital organs.

Accelerated hardening of the arteries of the brain, kidneys, and heart makes high blood pressure a major cause of strokes, kidney failure or uremia, and the lightning bolt of coronary occlusion. An even more closely related and frequent effect is a weakening of the heart muscle itself, which gradually grows "tired" of working against the circulatory resistance caused by hypertension. Then congestive heart failure occurs. When this begins to happen, salt restriction and the use of salt-excreting diuretics become a means not of prevention but of life preservation. Only with this help can the heart then continue to function well enough to maintain life. Even at this well-advanced point the restriction and increased excretion of salt is of such great help that comfortable living often can be maintained for many years.

Paradoxically, the most insidious threat of hypertension, per se, is that for many years, while it is slowly causing damage, it is a disease without symptoms. This is quite contrary to popular notions. Apparently this fact was known to William Shakespeare, who said, "This apoplexy . . . is a kind of lethargy . . . a kind of sleeping in the blood . . ." *(Henry IV, Part II)*. For this reason it is usually discovered accidentally during a routine checkup or an examination for another illness. It is a misconception that headaches or dizziness are clues to its presence, particularly during the early years. This misconception has been fostered because hypertension has often been found to be present when the patient goes to the doctor for headaches or other ill-defined symptoms that are entirely unrelated.

It has been shown recently by extensive surveys that at least half of the thirty or forty million people in the United States who have high blood pressure are completely unaware of it. It is even more disturbing to learn that almost two-thirds of those to whom the diagnosis is known are not receiving proper or adequate treatment. Many are getting no treatment at all! This shocking fact is largely due to the difficulty of getting someone who feels quite well to curtail severely the use of what to him and most Americans is an absolutely essential taste in his food. Besides giving that up he must, at least for some time, take a medication or medications that sometimes do cause mild or annoying symptoms, although previously he had none. Even if he at first complies, persuading this apparently well person to continue the sacrifice permanently presents the greatest obstacle to good treatment. Unless the physician is a master of his art, too often the patient gradually drops his salt restriction and medication. Since he continues to remain symptom-free, he rationalizes his initial fears, and the treatment becomes either sporadic or nonexistent. This is most unfortunate because the evidence is now rather convincing that even mild degrees of elevated blood pressure, unless relieved, can cause a statistically significant shortening of one's life span.

Hard facts regarding the actual cause of hypertension in over ninety percent of those who have it are still not known.

Yet the relationship of salt to its presence and its alleviation with salt removal has been well known for years. As long ago as the twenty-sixth century B.C. a Chinese savant said, "If too much salt is used in food the pulse hardens." In much more recent times a large body of valid scientific research has demonstrated conclusively that feeding salt to rats can produce hypertension on a direct, predictive, and quantitative basis. Quite reasonably no one has suggested that for absolute proof this should be checked out in humans, even on a small scale. So this remains indirect and circumstantial evidence. However, it should be kept in mind that practically all therapeutic and causative research is thoroughly and exhaustively performed first on animals. All of the modern miracles of medical science must pass such a stage before being applied to humans when cures of disease are being sought, but not usually causes.

In the course of these numerous salt-feeding experiments in rats, it was noted that a genetic or constitutional factor in a few lucky ones enabled them to resist the hypertensive effect not only of salt feeding but also of the insult of a variety of kidney conditions and of giving certain adrenal hormones. In the great majority, a combination of these environmental assaults together with this genetic predisposition led to varying degrees of hypertension, from mild to severe to fatal.

Population studies of large groups of people whose salt intake differed significantly yielded data that showed a clear-cut correlation between the average daily salt intake and the incidence of hypertension in many, but not all, groups. It was found, for example, that the people of the province of Akita in northern Japan had about the largest salt intake in the world, averaging twenty-five grams daily. About forty percent of this population also had hypertension! In southern Japan, around Hiroshima, the daily salt intake is about fourteen grams, and less than twenty percent of these people who are of the same race and genetic background as the northern Japanese are hypertensive.

On the other end of the scale the salt intake of Eskimos is about two grams daily, and hypertension in these people is practically unknown. Americans average ten to twelve grams of salt daily, and their incidence of hypertension is twelve percent to fifteen percent; Bantus of South Africa, eighteen grams daily with twenty-five percent hypertensive; Marshall Islanders seven grams daily with seven percent hypertensive.

We have clearly established a close relationship of salt intake to hypertension. Other valid observations indicate the effectiveness of salt deprivation in the control and treatment of hypertension and heart failure.

The problem, for which there have been a number of somewhat unsatisfactory solutions over the years, remains as to how a "salt-free" diet is best applied. Certainly not by means of the extreme monotony and rigidity of the Rice-Fruit Diet which, while quite effective, required such heroic self-sacrifice that it could be tolerated only by a few. This one drove everybody "up the wall" and in some cases actually off the roof! *Nor is a partial solution a satisfactory one.* Most patients for whom a low-sodium diet has been prescribed are not on low salt at all. They have not been given sufficiently specific instruction about which foods or food-products have an unknown, unapparent but naturally high content of sodium. It is not sufficient just to admonish against the obvious like pretzels, pickles, nuts, and salted butter.

Certainly few, if any at all, are given much instruction or even encouragement in replacing taste appeal to their new flat food through the use of many wonderful tasting herbs and spices. Small wonder the dismal statistic of non-compliance quoted earlier. I must confess I thought I was doing better than most with my instructions never to add salt in cooking or preparing food, to avoid milk and milk products, such as cheese, and to use processed foods rarely. This advice would be accompanied by a short list of foods that have a high natural content of sodium. The patient who carefully followed this advice probably reduced his salt intake to about two grams a day. Since the daily needs of the body normally do not exceed four grams and most of us use ten or twelve grams, this is not bad. We can and should decrease our sodium intake with more dietetic sophistication (knowledge plus elegance in taste), as is readily available in this book. From the patient's viewpoint, food appeal and taste have been almost completely ignored; they are really most important. When pressed on this matter, my suggestion has been to use lemon, garlic, and a "salt substitute." Salt substitutes contain potassium chloride as the substitute for sodium chloride and have the added benefit of being an excellent adjunct to diuretics. Unfortunately I have found patients do not readily accept them.

Recently one of the manufacturers told me that these substitutes give food better flavor if they are used in cooking and not sprinkled on like salt.

I believe this book and the information it contains should be "prescribed" whenever a low-salt or salt-free diet is dispensed by a physician. It should be prominently displayed on or near the prescription counter of every drugstore alongside other long-established, self-applicable over-the-counter therapies such as Aspirin or Tums. It is wholly representative of my personal therapeutic philosophy that health prohibitions and admonitions do not have to be a matter of hard deprivation versus dire consequences. It need not be a "Do without, or else!" For the diabetic and obese, there are excellent artificial sweeteners; for the coronary-prone, there are an increasing number of foods in which cholesterol has been removed or replaced by unsaturated fats; and for the salt-deprived, there is an abundance of wonderful recipes with natural herbs and spices, à la Roth!

Wise is the physician who teaches his patients that the best and healthiest life is a series of intelligent compromises.

S. K. Fineberg, M.D., F.A.C.P., F.(A)A.C.C.

Clinical Associate Professor of Medicine,
    New York Medical College

Chief, Diabetes and Obesity-Diabetes
    Clinics, Metropolitan Hospital, New York City

Director of Medicine and Cardiologist,
    Prospect Hospital, Bronx, N.Y.

Dear Reader:

Salt-free cooking does not mean the end of enjoyment of food but rather the beginning of a study of how to make food enjoyable. This book has been written to make that study easier for those who have doctor's orders to restrict their intake of sodium. It's important that this be done with medical direction rather than as a self-prescribed health measure, although much can be learned from this book about sensible patterns of eating for the whole family.

The problem of cooking for a special-diet patient is that it usually creates chaos in the kitchen. The recipes in this book are constructed to please the patient but can easily feed the rest of the household if a saltshaker is passed to them at the table, eliminating the need for separate pots and pans.

If you are not the patient but are cooking for someone who is, be sure to have him or her read the book too. Much can be learned from the facts of low-sodium cooking to help the patient adhere to this kind of diet restriction. The patient can study the list of natural sodium content in foods at the end of chapter 1, as well as read up on what may be ordered when dining out (chapter 2). Understanding the facts can be a matter of life and health in cases of serious hypertension or kidney disease and also can be helpful to coronary patients and those suffering from obesity.

Not a grain of salt has been used in any of the recipes, but the wizardry of herbs and spices transforms otherwise bland dishes into delectable ones. This book has been a labor of caring about your particular diet problems, and I hope it helps you to resolve them.

Sincerely,

*June Roth*

# Salt-Free Cooking with Herbs and Spices

# 1

# What the Doctor's Order of No Salt Really Means

Don't despair when the doctor prescribes a salt-free diet for you or a member of your family. You will be trading a saltshaker for a new gamut of cooking with herbs and spices that will provide subtle flavors and fine dining.

Many of the recipes you already have may need only slight alteration to remain in use, as you reexamine them for sodium content. Others will have to be discarded for the time being, while new recipes are put into use to follow the doctor's orders. This book is designed to create delicious meals that compensate for the medical restrictions.

It is best to have a conference with the doctor to find out exactly what kind of salt-free program he has in mind. It is likely that he will recommend a *mild sodium-restricted diet*, which permits a reduction of sodium intake to about half the normal usage. The goal will probably be to restrict the patient to between 2500 and 3000 milligrams of sodium.

To accomplish this, remove the saltshaker from the table and avoid the use of salt or monosodium glutamate in cooking. Some doctors will recommend the elimination of salt or monosodium glutamate in cooking altogether, while others may be a little lenient. The recipes in this book do not depend on the use of any sodium additives for flavoring or baking, but special medications for the patient might make it possible to follow a less strict regime. In any event, the amounts of salt and monosodium glutamate will have to be either eliminated completely or cut down drastically, and clarification from the doctor of these amounts is a most important point.

1

In addition to resolving specific instructions for the use of salt, avoid all foods preserved in brine, all canned vegetables, soups, fish, and prepared dinners. If you do this, you will not have to worry about the sodium content of regular baked bread, pasta, milk, and natural meats and vegetables. The patient should be alerted to the high sodium content of catsup, prepared mustard, commercial mayonnaise, soy sauce, and Worcestershire sauce. Small quantities of cheese may be allowed, but avoid all salty snacks such as potato chips, pretzels, and salted nuts.

In comparison to more rigid diets, the prescription for a mild sodium-restricted diet is just a slight tap on the wrist, telling you to watch labels carefully and to avoid a large intake of all additives that have the word *sodium* in them. This includes those words that have *soda* as part of their title and those labels that include the chemical symbol *Na*. It is the least restrictive kind of low-sodium diet and one that is relatively easy to follow.

However, the doctor may have reason to be more specific and strict with his recommendations and may prefer you to follow a 1000-milligram sodium diet, a 500-milligram sodium diet, or a rigid 250-milligram sodium diet. Do not follow the more rigid diets without a definite order to do so. The slap on the wrist gets harder as the numbers decrease.

**1000-MILLIGRAM SODIUM DIET:** You can figure that about 500 milligrams of sodium, or half of the amount, is eaten as the natural content of basic foods each day. The other half will have to be carefully regulated so that you do not add more than 500 milligrams of sodium to your food and drink each day. Remember that water and medicines have sodium content and must be included in your daily total. This might require some investigative work on your part with your pharmacist and with your local health department. The doctor will eliminate the use of salt and monosodium glutamate completely from the diet of the patient. This is understandable because ¼ teaspoon of salt contains 575 milligrams of sodium. You can refer to the chart at the end of this chapter to find out how much sodium is contained in raw foods. This will enable you to plan menus that will not exceed 1000 milligrams of sodium, if this is what the doctor has prescribed.

If you are using an artificial sweetener, be sure that the kind you use is without sodium. Use unsalted butter or margarine and avoid all commercial products with a listing of any kind of sodium. The following is a list of such sodium compounds that are common additives to the food you purchase and that are prohibited on a sodium-restricted diet:

**Sodium chloride**—salt used in cooking, canning, and processing.

**Monosodium glutamate**—MSG, a seasoning used in home and restaurant cooking, and in many packaged, canned, and processed frozen foods.

**Baking powder**—used in the preparation of breads and cakes.

**Baking soda**—sodium bicarbonate or bicarbonate of soda, used in the preparation of breads, cakes, and sometimes added to vegetable cookery; also is used as an alkalizer for cases of indigestion.

**Brine**—salt and water solution used in processing foods, and in canning, freezing, and pickling.

**Disodium phosphate**—used in some quick-cooking cereals and in processed cheeses.

**Sodium alginate**—used in chocolate milks and ice creams for smooth texture.

**Sodium benzoate**—used as a preservative in condiments.

**Sodium hydroxide**—used in food processing of some fruits and vegetables, hominy, and ripe olives.

**Sodium propionate**—used in pasteurized cheeses and in some breads and cakes.

**Sodium sulfite**—used as a bleach for some fresh fruits and as a preservative of some dried fruits.

Do not use canned products, unless they are labeled *salt free.* Do not use baking powder or baking soda in your food preparations. Instead, you may substitute cream of tartar, potassium bicarbonate, sodium-free baking powder, and yeast. Avoid carbonated beverages, all convenience food mixes, molasses, commercial candies, malted milk, instant cocoa mixes, smoked meats, frozen fish, salted cottage cheese, all cheeses that are not labeled *low-sodium dietetic*, salted crackers and snacks, cereals with salt additives, and self-rising flour or self-rising cornmeal.

Look at labels to determine whether frozen vegetables are processed with salt. Pay particular attention to peas and lima beans, which are often lightly salted. Do not use the following vegetables in any form because they are high in natural sodium: artichokes, beets and beet greens, carrots, celery, swiss chard, dandelion greens, hominy, kale, mustard greens, spinach, and white turnips. Small amounts of the preceding vegetables may be used in the preparation of a recipe to give flavor, if the patient does not eat them. Use only unsalted breads, rolls, and crackers.

**500-MILLIGRAM SODIUM DIET:** You will have to be even more restrictive in your use of sodium and may need the help of a nutrition expert to plan your menus. Your doctor may want you to use low-sodium milk. You will certainly need to check on the sodium content of your water supply—if there are not more than 5 milligrams of sodium in 8 ounces of water, you will not have to use distilled water. Otherwise you may have to use distilled water for drinking and cooking. Do not use softened water, whether it is city supplied or home processed, as it usually contains too much sodium for the 500-milligram sodium diet.

**250-MILLIGRAM SODIUM DIET:** Besides all the preceding information you will need careful calculations to meet the restrictions of this diet. Just as you have learned how to count calories of food, so you may have to learn how to count milligrams of sodium to be able to follow your doctor's orders. There are about 2300 milligrams of sodium in 1 level teaspoon of salt, so you can readily see why the elimination of all salt in cooking will produce a rapid decline in the sodium intake of the patient. But just stopping the use of salt at the table and in cooking is not enough if you are on a 1000-milligram, or lower, sodium-restricted diet. You must learn to choose foods wisely, as all foods contain some sodium. Meat, fish, eggs, and milk have more natural sodium than fruits, vegetables, and cereals. The size of the portions allowed of the foods with a higher sodium content will depend on the type of diet your doctor prescribes.

The following is a sodium chart to help you make your selections intelligently.

## FOODS HIGH IN SODIUM
(Not allowed on any sodium-restricted diet)

Anchovies
Bacon and bacon fat
Beef, chipped
Beef, corned
Bouillon cubes (unless salt free)
Catsup
Caviar
Celery salt
Cheese (all kinds, unless low-sodium)
Chili sauce
Cod, dried
Fish, salted and smoked
Frankfurters
Garlic salt
Herring
Luncheon meats
Meat extracts
Meat sauces
Meat tenderizers
Meats, salted and smoked
Mustard, prepared
Nuts, salted
Olives
Onion salt
Pickles
Popcorn, salted
Potato chips
Pretzels
Relishes
Salt at the table
Salt pork
Sardines
Sausages
Sauerkraut
Soy sauce
Worcestershire sauce

## FOODS MODERATELY HIGH IN SODIUM

(Not allowed on a 1000-, or 500- or 250-mg. sodium-restricted diets)

Baking powder
Baking soda
Beets and beet greens
Beverage mixes
Bread, rolls, and crackers
    (regular)
Butter, salted
Carrots
Celery
Clams
Crabs
Dandelion greens
Fish, canned (regular)
Kale
Kidneys
Lobster

Meats, canned (regular)
Margarine, salted
Molasses
Mustard greens
Oysters
Salad dressings (regular)
Scallops
Shrimp
Spinach
Swiss Chard
Vegetables, canned (reg-
    ular)
Vegetable juices, canned
    (regular)
Waffles

## APPROXIMATE SODIUM CONTENT OF COMMON FOODS

| Food | Measure | Approximate Mg. Sodium |
|------|---------|------------------------|
| **Meats, Poultry, Fish, and Eggs** | | |
| Beef, veal* | 3 ounces | 75 |
| Lamb, pork* | 3 ounces | 75 |
| Ham (cured)* | 3 ounces | 675 |
| Bacon* | 1 slice | 675 |
| Frankfurter* | 1 whole | 540 |
| Bologna | 1 slice | 390 |
| Chicken* | 3 ounces | 75 |
| Egg | 1 whole | 60 |
| Fish (fresh, excluding shellfish)* | 3 ounces | 75 |

*Amounts listed are for cooked weight, without bone.

# APPROXIMATE SODIUM CONTENT OF COMMON FOODS

| Food | Measure | Approximate Mg. Sodium |
|---|---|---|
| **Nuts** | | |
| Peanuts, salted | ¼ cup | 275 |
| Peanuts, unsalted | ¼ cup | 2 |
| | | |
| **Vegetables**\*\* | | |
| Asparagus, corn, cucumber, eggplant, green beans, green pepper, lima beans, okra, onions, peas, potatoes, pumpkin, rutabaga, squash, sweet potatoes, tomato. | 1 cup | 5 |
| Broccoli, brussels sprouts, cabbage, cauliflower, lettuce, radishes, turnip greens, dry beans. | ½ cup | 15 |
| Beets, carrots, celery, kale, spinach, turnips | ½ cup | 40 |

\*\*Amounts listed are for fresh and canned foods, or for frozen foods without sodium or salt.

## APPROXIMATE SODIUM CONTENT OF COMMON FOODS

| Food | Measure | Approximate Mg. Sodium |
|------|---------|------------------------|
| **Fruits** All (excluding raisins and cantaloupe) | ½ cup | 2 |
| Raisins | ½ cup | 15 |
| Cantaloupe | ½ medium | 25 |
| **Breads and Cereals** | | |
| Wheat germ | ¼ cup | 5 |
| Puffed wheat, puffed rice, shredded wheat | 1 cup | 1 |
| Corn flakes | 1 cup | 165 |
| Bran flakes | ¾ cup | 340 |
| Whole wheat bread | 1 slice | 170 |
| White bread (enriched) | 1 slice | 170 |
| Macaroni | ½ cup cooked | 1 |
| Rice | ½ cup cooked | 3 |
| **Dairy products** | | |
| Low fat milk | 1 cup | 120 |
| Buttermilk | 1 cup | 225 |
| Cheese—cheddar, Muenster, Swiss, American | 1 ounce | 220 |
| Cottage cheese, creamed | ¼ cup | 160 |

## APPROXIMATE SODIUM CONTENT OF COMMON FOODS

| Food | Measure | Approximate Mg. Sodium |
|---|---|---|
| Cottage cheese, unsalted | ¼ cup | 30 |
| Parmesan cheese | 1 tablespoon | 40 |
| Low-fat cheese—sapsago, tilsiter, port salut | 1 ounce | 200 |
| **Other items** | | |
| Margarine, salted | 1 tablespoon | 110 |
| Margarine, unsalted | 1 tablespoon | 1 |
| Green olive | 1 whole | 155 |
| Dill pickle | 1 large | 1400 |
| Salt | ¼ teaspoon | 575 |
| Catsup | 1 tablespoon | 890 |
| Worcestershire sauce | 1 tablespoon | 815 |
| Peanut butter (regular) | 1 tablespoon | 18 |
| Gelatin, plain | 1 tablespoon | 8 |
| Gelatin, flavored | 1 box (4-5 servings) | 830 |

# 2

# What About Dining Out?

Eating out may present one of the greatest problems to the sodium-restricted dieter, but it can be solved. If you have accepted invitations to a private home, be sure to advise the hostess of the diet restriction and ask that she prepare a platter for the patient that will follow the doctor's orders. If you are following a mildly restricted low-sodium prescription, simply explain and request that the salt and MSG seasoning be limited to half the normal amount if it is a one-dish casserole. Suggest that a broiled piece of fish, chicken, or beef be substituted if the hostess is planning a high-sodium main course, and don't be embarrassed about being served something different from the other guests. If it is done quietly, it should not upset the congeniality of the dinner.

Restaurants by contrast are less of a problem. Avoid all prepared foods that have to be heavily salted to taste good. Choose grapefruit, fresh fruit cup, and similar fare for starters—avoiding all baked clams, antipasto, everything sauced, and all soups. For main courses, tell the waiter to inform the chef that no salt or MSG may be used on your food. Then order broiled chops or steak; an inside cut of roast beef, lamb, or pork with no gravy; sliced turkey with no gravy; broiled chicken or fish; baked potato; and a salad instead of the vegetables offered. Ask for no dressing with the salad but request a cruet of oil and vinegar. If that is not available, ask for several slices of lemon and squeeze them on the salad instead. An accommodating chef might slip a half of tomato with a sprinkling of oregano under the broiler for you. All prepared vegetables that are ready in the steamers have been seasoned with salt and should not be ordered.

Avoid dining in Oriental restaurants, unless you know that the chef will prepare a special dish without the usual heavy-handed addition of MSG to heighten flavors.

You can dine in an Italian restaurant if you order fettuccini cooked in salt-free water and tossed with sweet butter. If you are on a mildly restricted low-sodium diet you may add a tablespoon of grated Parmesan cheese at the table—for 1000-mg., or lower, sodium restrictions, skip the cheese and have another glass of wine. Don't order the chicken cacciatore, veal Parmigiana or other sauced main dishes. Instead ask the chef to prepare salt-free veal piccata with thin slices of lemon—delicate and delicious. Unless you have arranged in advance for the chef to prepare a special salt-free sauce, avoid choosing anything with a regular sauce because it probably has a base of canned tomatoes and tomato paste, which are high in sodium content.

Most airlines will provide a low-sodium meal if advised in advance. If not, be sure to pack some sustenance for the trip and avoid the problem of hunger pangs while everyone around you is dining on one of those Barbie doll dinners.

If a lunch bag from home fits in with your work style, carry a bag, the easiest way to insure your diet maintenance. If you lunch out, try to order broiled fish or chicken with no sauce, or a chef's salad with only sliced chicken, instructing the waiter to leave out the cheese and ham. If you take coffee breaks, watch carefully what you munch on with your beverage. Here too, you'd be better off to pack a snack to take with you.

With a lot of determination and a little ingenuity, it is possible to adhere to low-sodium restrictions and still enjoy dining out. You merely have to read the menu with a sodium detective's eyes.

# 3

# Herbs and Spices to the Rescue

$A$ low-sodium prescribed diet will certainly lead you to explore the wonderful world of herbs and spices. Every cook is familiar with the more popular of these in conjunction with the usual salt and pepper additives to flavor food. But when the saltshaker is taken away, it's important to learn about all the flavor enhancers you may substitute. Soon you will not miss the salt as the subtle skill of herb and spice cookery prevails.

To differentiate between the two, *herbs* are aromatic leaves and *spices* are pungent seeds that are usually crushed to provide taste bud sensations. Each has a special affinity for certain foods, and some work particularly well together. All should be used in small quantities in the beginning. If using fresh herbs rather than the dried variety, use about three to four times the amount recommended in the recipe. Keep all containers tightly covered and replace herbs and spices with fresh supplies if they lose their aroma or color.

You may be inspired to start an indoor or outdoor herb garden. If so, remember that your excess leaf clippings may be stored in small airtight plastic bags or containers and kept in the freezer. Or they may be gathered into small bunches in airtight containers at room temperature.

The more you get to know about herbs and spices, the wider variety of flavors you will be able to attain without salt. Here is a specially prepared chart to help you choose the right herbs and spices for each dish.

| HERBS AND SPICES | CHARACTERISTICS | COMPATIBILITY |
|---|---|---|
| Allspice | A sharply flavored berry, dried and ground into a powder that tastes like a combination of cinnamon and cloves. | Fruit, fruit pies, and some meat dishes. |
| Basil | A member of the mint family with a sweet-flavored leaf. | Tomatoes, soups, salads, and Italian-style sauces. Good in some meat stews. |
| Bay Leaf | A dried leaf of the laurel family with a strong aromatic flavor. | Use with stewed meats and hearty soups. |
| Caraway | Small aromatic seeds of a parsley-type plant. | Use to flavor breads, cheese, cabbage dishes, and some meat dishes. |
| Cardamom | A ground or whole seed that is a member of the ginger family, characterized by a sweet and pungent flavor. | Used in Indian and Scandinavian cooking—in curries and in pastries. |
| Cayenne | This is also called red pepper or chili pepper. It is ground into a powder from the fruit of the capsicum plant. The powder has a hot, biting taste. | Use sparingly in some meat dishes, cheese dishes, and spicy sauces. |

| | | |
|---|---|---|
| **Chervil** | Has an anise flavor and is a member of the parsley family. | Use in soups, egg dishes, carrots, peas, and spinach. |
| **Chili Powder** | A powdered blend of chili pepper, oregano, cumin, and garlic, sometimes with cloves and allspice added. | Enhances Mexican cooking. Use in sauces, stews, and meat dishes. |
| **Chives** | Hollow green tips of an onion-family plant with a subtle onion taste. | Use in salads, with sour cream for baked potatoes, in delicate sauces, and in some cheese dishes. Use with beans, cauliflower, mushrooms, peas, potatoes, and tomatoes. |
| **Cinnamon** | Has an aromatic, sweet-pungent taste; is available in stick form or ground into a fine powder. Made from the bark of several trees, including the cassia in the U.S. | Use in fruit pies and compotes, in Middle Eastern meat dishes, with sweet potatoes, yellow squash, apples, apricots, blueberries, cherries, cranberries, figs, grapefruit, peaches, pears, pineapple, plums, prunes, and rhubarb. |

**Cloves**

An aromatic, pungent-tasting dried bud hat is available whole or ground. Has a warm spicy flavor.

Use in pickled dishes, ham, tongue, desserts, mulled wines, and teas. Use with beets, cabbage, carrots, yellow squash, apples, apricots, blueberries, cherries, cranberries, lemon, lime, peaches, pears, plums, prunes, and rhubarb.

**Coriander**

A member of the parsley family, it is usually in leaf form. Its seeds have a lemon-sage flavor and can also be used.

Use in salads, soups, and stews. Use seeds in curries, pastries, and some meat dishes. Use with artichokes and tomatoes.

**Cumin**

A nutty-flavored seed related to the parsley family and available whole or ground. Is often an ingredient of chili powder and curry powder.

Use in Middle Eastern recipes for soups, cabbage dishes, fish and meat dishes. Also use with corn and cucumbers.

**Curry Powder**

A blend of many spices ground together, including cayenne, coriander, cumin, turmeric, and sometimes allspice, cinnamon, ginger, and pepper, creating a hot, spicy flavor.

Use in Indian-style cooking, for soups, sauces, stews, and seafood dishes. Use with beans, broccoli, brussels sprouts, cabbage, corn, onions, potatoes, and summer squash.

**Dill**

A member of the parsley family with a distinct odor and flavor. The stem and leaves are available as "dillweed" and the seeds as "dillseed."

Use in pickling, soups, seafood and chicken dishes, and cream sauces. Use to flavor beans, beets, brussels sprouts, cabbage, carrots, eggplant, potatoes, spinach, tomatoes, and white turnips.

**Garlic**

A bulb with many cloves that has a strong and distinct odor and flavor. Also available in powder or salt form.

Rub a cut clove on a wooden salad bowl for subtle flavor. Use to season meats, seafood, chicken, and sauces. Use with onions, mushrooms, potatoes, and tomatoes.

**Ginger**

Has a sweet and spicy flavor and is obtained from the root of a tropical plant. Available in slivers or ground.

Use to flavor cooked fruits, pastry, sauces, some Far Eastern meat dishes. Use with carrots, onions, peas, sweet potatoes, apples, cherries, cranberries, figs, grapefruit, peaches, pears, pineapple, and rhubarb.

**Mace**

A powder ground from the membrane of the fruit of the nutmeg tree with a flavor similar to nutmeg—warm and spicy but a little more pungent. It is not as deep in color as nutmeg.

Use in baking, sauces, pumpkin dishes, and in some meat and fish dishes. Use as a seasoning with carrots, potatoes, spinach, sweet potatoes, apples, peaches, and pineapple.

**Marjoram**  A member of the mint family, this leaf has a sweet, tangy taste and is available whole or ground.  Use in soups, lamb dishes, and in stuffings. Use with asparagus, beets, brussels sprouts, carrots, celery, onions, peas, spinach, summer squash, tomatoes, and zucchini.

**Mint**  An aromatic herb of the mint family, most popularly known as spearmint.  Use in jellies, sauces, candies, meat dishes, and some desserts. Use with beans, beets, carrots, peas, potatoes, spinach, melon, oranges, and pineapple.

**Mustard**  Prepared from the mustard seed in powdered or paste form, it has a hot, sharp flavor.  Use in cheese, meat, and fish dishes, as a condiment for sandwiches, and with cabbage, celery, cucumber pickles, peas, and spinach.

**Nutmeg**  A seed with a sweet, spicy flavor that is available in whole or ground form.  Use in baking, puddings, sauces, meat dishes, and with asparagus, beans, beets, broccoli, brussels sprouts, cabbage, carrots, cauliflower, onions, peas, spinach, summer squash, apples, blueberries, cherries, cranberries, lemon, lime, pineapple, and rhubarb.

| | | |
|---|---|---|
| **Oregano** | A member of the mint family. Leaf has a strong but pleasantly bitter taste. | Use in Italian and Mexican cooking, in tomato sauces, eggs, cheese, and meat dishes. Use with beans, broccoli, eggplant, mushrooms, onions, peas, spinach, tomatoes, and zucchini. |
| **Paprika** | A fine, red powder with a slightly sweet taste, made from the fruit of a variety of red pepper. It is used both to decorate and flavor food. | Use with Hungarian cooking, on roasts, poultry, eggs, and in soups. Use with corn, cauliflower, onions, and potatoes. |
| **Parsley** | Aromatic-tasting leaves are available fresh, dried, and are used either as a garnish and for seasoning. | Use for fish, meat, soups, sauces, and with asparagus, beets, eggplant, mushrooms, potatoes, tomatoes, and zucchini. |
| **Pepper** | A dried pungent berry that is available in whole form, known as "peppercorns" or ground. Black pepper is obtained from the entire berry and has a more intense taste, while white pepper is ground after the outer covering has been removed from the seed. | Use for soups, sauces, meats, poultry, fish, and with beans, cabbage, celery, eggplant, onions, peas, potatoes, spinach, tomatoes, and zucchini. |

| | | |
|---|---|---|
| **Rosemary** | Sweet-flavored leaf of the mint family. Is used dried or fresh. | Use in lamb dishes, sauces, soups, and with carrots, cauliflower, eggplant, mushrooms, onions, peas, potatoes, spinach, summer squash, white turnips, and yellow turnips. |
| **Saffron** | Made from the dried golden stigmas of a variety of crocus. It is used sparingly for its slightly bitter taste and as a yellow coloring agent for food. | Use in Spanish, French, and Italian dishes that contain rice. Also use in some sauces and soups. |
| **Sage** | Member of the mint family with leaves that have a pungent, slightly bitter taste. May be dried or ground. | Use to season stuffings, soups, sauces, and meat dishes. Adds distinction to vinegar marinades. Use with brussels sprouts, eggplant, onions, potatoes, summer squash, and tomatoes. |
| **Savory** | A member of the mint family. Summer savory is more subtle in taste than winter savory, which has a thymelike flavor. | Use in egg cookery and in sauces. Use with asparagus, beans, brussels sprouts, eggplant, and yellow turnips. |

| **Tarragon** | Aromatic leaves that have a slightly licorice flavor. | Use to enhance sauces, eggs, chicken, and some meat dishes. Use with asparagus, beets, cabbage, mushrooms, and tomatoes. |
| --- | --- | --- |
| **Thyme** | A member of the mint family with a warm, aromatic flavor. | Use in chowders, stuffings, and in some cheese and fruit dishes. Use with asparagus, beans, beets, carrots, eggplant, mushrooms, onions, potatoes, spinach, tomatoes, white turnips, yellow turnips, and zucchini. |
| **Turmeric** | A member of the ginger family; an important ingredient of curry powder. | Use in curries, fish dishes, and sauces; use for pickling. Use to season cauliflower, peas, and tomatoes. |

# 4

# Salt-Free Appetizers

COCKTAIL nibbles and first courses don't have to be dull fare for the low-sodium patient. Those on a mild sodium-restricted diet will be able to pick and choose from regularly prepared offerings—avoiding all cheese, ham, bacon, frankfurters, bologna, salami, and similar high-sodium foods. Don't touch salted popcorn, pretzels, potato chips, corn chips, salted nuts, or any pickled foods. Ignore all mixed dips, especially those with a dried onion soup base. Enjoy a small amount of shellfish, meatballs, broiled mushrooms, pâtés, fresh raw vegetables, and any fruit in sight.

Those restricted to a 1000-, 500-, or 250-mg. low-sodium diet will have to be even more careful. When in doubt about an appetizer, ask what the ingredients are. If salt, MSG, Worcestershire sauce, soy sauce, garlic salt, onion salt, or any catsup, chili sauce, or prepared mustard have been used, do not eat it. Be sure not to touch the shellfish, and avoid raw carrots in the vegetable offerings.

Order straight liquors or wine without a carbonated mixer. Vodka or gin with orange juice is all right, but with tomato juice (unless it is low-sodium) it is not. Follow your doctor's orders on the limitations of drinks allowed, as certain conditions may preclude having any drinks at all.

You will find the recipes in this chapter to be deceptively delicious. Many may be served as a first course for dinner and all may be served to guests with confidence. The salt may be out, but the taste is definitely in.

# Avocado Dip

1 mashed ripe avocado
½ cup finely chopped tomato
1 tablespoon finely minced onion
¼ cup blender mayonnaise (see index)
2 teaspoons lemon juice
  A few drops liquid hot pepper seasoning

Mix mashed avocado, chopped tomato, minced onion, mayonnaise, and lemon juice until well blended. Add hot pepper seasoning. Refrigerate until chilled. Serve as a dip with unsalted crackers.

*Makes 1½ cups.*

*This recipe may be used for all low-sodium diets. Those restricted to 1000-, 500-, or 250-mg. low-sodium diets should not eat carrot or celery sticks. Those restricted to 500- or 250-mg. low-sodium diets should substitute low-sodium milk for regular milk.*

# Raw Vegetable Dip

1 cup low-sodium cottage cheese
½ teaspoon garlic powder
¼ teaspoon white pepper
⅛ teaspoon thyme
  Milk

Place cottage cheese, garlic powder, pepper, and thyme in an electric blender. Blend until mixture is creamy. Add milk by the tablespoonful to thin the mixture. (Keep mixture just thick enough to adhere to the raw vegetables.) Serve with a platter of raw cauliflower florets, raw cucumber sticks, raw carrot sticks, and raw celery sticks.

*Makes 1 cup dip.*

# Chopped Eggplant

1 eggplant
1 sliced onion
1 green pepper, cut up
1 tablespoon oil
¼ teaspoon pepper
¼ teaspoon thyme
1 tablespoon lemon juice
  Unsalted crackers or lettuce leaves (optional)

Preheat oven to 350° F. Bake the whole eggplant until skin is soft and wrinkled. Remove from oven and cut skin away. Chop in a large chopping bowl. Add onion and green pepper and chop all very fine. Add oil, pepper, thyme, and lemon juice. Mix well and refrigerate. Serve cold on lettuce leaves as an appetizer or salad, or serve with crackers as a spread.

*Makes about 2 cups.*

# Hot Puffs

1 cup blender mayonnaise (see index)
¼ teaspoon dry mustard
1 teaspoon finely chopped dill
1 egg white
24 unsalted round crackers

Combine mayonnaise, mustard, and dill. Beat egg white until stiff and fold into the mayonnaise mixture. Spoon onto crackers. Slip under the broiler for a minute or two until lightly browned.

*Makes 2 dozen.*

## Cottage-Cheese-Stuffed Mushrooms

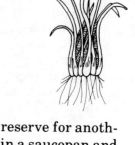

24 large fresh mushrooms
½ cup low-sodium cottage cheese
½ teaspoon powdered garlic
1 tablespoon chopped chives
¼ teaspoon thyme
⅛ teaspoon paprika

Wash mushrooms; remove stems and reserve for another use. Cover mushroom caps with water in a saucepan and cook for about 15 minutes, covered. Drain and chill. Combine cottage cheese, garlic, chives, and thyme. Spoon mixture into mushroom caps. Sprinkle with paprika. Chill again.

*Makes 2 dozen.*

## Pickled Mushrooms

1 pound uniform-sized small mushrooms
¼ cup tarragon vinegar
¼ teaspoon oregano
2 whole peppercorns

Wash and dry mushrooms; trim ends of the stems. Place the whole mushrooms in a clean container and add tarragon vinegar, oregano, and peppercorns. Cover and toss well. Refrigerate for several days, shaking occasionally to distribute marinade. Remove mushrooms from liquid just before serving. Place on lettuce leaves for an appetizer course, or serve with picks as an hors d'oeuvre.

*Makes 8 servings as an appetizer.*

# Broiled Dates

¾ cup soft brown sugar
½ cup water
¼ cup lemon juice
¼ cup cider vinegar
1 teaspoon grated orange rind
½ teaspoon cinnamon
¼ teaspoon nutmeg
1 package (8-ounces) pitted dates

Combine sugar, water, lemon juice, vinegar, orange rind, cinnamon, and nutmeg in a heavy saucepan. Place over medium heat, stirring until sugar dissolves. Bring mixture to a boil; reduce heat and simmer 5 minutes. Place dates in small glass bowl; pour hot mixture over dates. Cover and place on rack to cool. Refrigerate at least 24 hours to allow flavors to blend. Drain dates. Place in the broiler in a broiling pan and broil about 3 minutes. Serve hot with picks.

*Makes about 3 dozen appetizers.*

# Broiled Chicken Livers

1 pound fresh chicken livers
¼ cup orange marmalade
2 tablespoons unsalted butter or margarine
¼ teaspoon dry mustard
¼ teaspoon ginger

Cut each chicken liver in half. Combine marmalade, butter, mustard, and ginger in a small saucepan; heat and stir until butter is melted and well blended. Dip each piece of liver into the mixture to coat; then place in the broiler on a broiling pan. Broil for 5 minutes or until done. Serve hot with picks.

*Makes about 2 dozen appetizers.*

# Swedish Meat Balls

1 pound ground beef
½ pound ground pork
1 cup mashed potatoes
1 egg
2 tablespoons minced onion
1 teaspoon sugar
¼ teaspoon pepper
¼ teaspoon nutmeg
⅛ teaspoon allspice
⅛ teaspoon ginger
¼ cup unsalted butter or margarine

Combine ground beef and ground pork. Add mashed potatoes. Stir in egg, onion, sugar, pepper, nutmeg, allspice, and ginger; mix thoroughly. Form into tiny balls using about 1 tablespoon of mixture per ball. Melt butter in a large skillet; add meatballs and brown over low heat, shaking pan occasionally to brown evenly.

*Makes about 4 dozen meatballs.*

# Curried Pâté Balls

1 cup unsalted butter or margarine
½ teaspoon curry powder
½ cup finely diced onion
2 pounds chicken livers
1 cup chopped unsalted walnuts
2 tablespoons chopped dried parsley
  Unsalted crackers

Heat 1/3 cup of the butter with curry powder in a skillet until it forms bubbles; add onion and chicken livers. Cook slowly until livers lose their pinkness and are done. Mash or sieve contents of skillet, beating in 1/3 cup butter until entire mixture is smooth and well blended. Chill several hours or overnight to firm mixture. Shape into about 36 balls the size of a walnut; roll each ball in chopped walnuts. Sprinkle with chopped parsley. Just before serving, heat remaining 1/3 cup butter in a chafing dish; add chicken liver balls and heat quickly. Serve hot with crackers.

*Makes 3 dozen balls.*

 *This recipe may be used for all low-sodium diets. Those restricted to 500- or 250-mg. low-sodium diets should substitute low-sodium bread for regular bread.*

## Lamb Toasties

¼ cup blender mayonnaise (see index)
1 small minced onion
¼ teaspoon paprika
2 tablespoons chopped chives
1 teaspoon lemon juice
½ pound cooked ground lamb
14 slices white bread
¼ cup melted unsalted butter or margarine
2 tablespoons sesame seeds
  Parsley

Preheat oven to 425° F. Blend together mayonnaise, onion, paprika, chives, and lemon juice. Add ground lamb. Trim crusts from bread. Cut each slice into three equal strips. Brush one side with butter and sprinkle with sesame seeds. Place on a baking sheet. Bake for 8 to 10 minutes or until lightly browned. Turn and brown the other side. Spread the lamb mixture on toast strips. Garnish with parsley and serve cold, or return the toasties to the oven for several minutes and serve piping hot.

*Makes 3½ dozen appetizers.*

# Shrimp Provençale

4 tablespoons unsalted butter or margarine
1 peeled garlic clove
1 pound small shrimp, shelled and deveined
1 thinly sliced green onion
4 whole peppercorns
2 tablespoons chopped parsley

Melt butter in a skillet. Put the garlic clove on a skewer and add it to the skillet with shrimp, onion, peppercorns, and parsley. Stir occasionally, and as steam comes up, cover, and simmer gently over low heat for 5 to 10 minutes or until shrimp turn pink. Remove garlic clove. Serve with cocktail picks, hot or cold.

*Makes about 8 servings.*

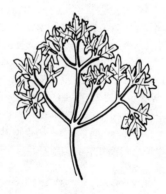

*This recipe may be used for mild sodium-restricted diets only. Those restricted to 1000-, 500-, or 250-mg. low-sodium diets should omit this recipe.*

# Pickled Shrimp

**1 cup tarragon vinegar**
**¼ cup water**
**1 tablespoon sugar**
**3 cloves**
**1 bay leaf**
**1 peeled garlic clove**
**⅛ teaspoon pepper**
**1 sliced onion**
**1 pound cooked shrimp, shelled and deveined**

Combine the vinegar, water, sugar, cloves, bay leaf, garlic, pepper, and sliced onion in a saucepan; bring to a boil. Place the cooked shrimp in a one-quart jar and cover with the hot marinade. Place a tight lid on the jar and refrigerate overnight or for as long as two days. Drain and serve with toothpicks.

*Makes about 8 servings.*

# Broiled Honeyed Grapefruit

**2 grapefruits, halved**
**4 teaspoons honey**
**½ teaspoon cinnamon**

Cut around the edges and sections of grapefruit halves. Drizzle the top of each half with a teaspoon of honey and ⅛ teaspoon cinnamon. Broil grapefruit for about 6 minutes or until browned. Serve hot.

*Makes 4 servings.*

# Curried Fruit

SAUCE:

¼ **cup chopped onion**
1 **minced garlic clove**
2 **teaspoons curry powder**
½ **teaspoon ground ginger**
½ **teaspoon dry mustard**
¼ **teaspoon pepper**
2 **tablespoons wine vinegar**
1 **tablespoon lemon juice**
1½ **teaspoons honey**
½ **tomato, skinned and seeded**

To prepare the sauce, in a large saucepan mix together the onion, garlic, curry, ginger, mustard, pepper, vinegar, lemon juice, and honey. Place the tomato in an electric blender and process at high speed; add to the saucepan. Place the sauce over low heat, cover, and simmer for 15 minutes. Let the sauce cool while the fruit is prepared.

FRUIT BOWL:

2 **cored and cubed apples**
2 **cored and cubed pears**
1½ **cups halved and seeded grapes**
6 **bananas**

In a large bowl, combine apples, pears, and grapes. Peel and slice the bananas and add to the fruit bowl. Lightly toss. Add the curry sauce just before serving.

*Makes 6 servings.*

# 5

# Salt-Free Soups

SAY good-bye to all condensed canned soups and dehydrated soup mixes when you have been ordered to adhere to a low sodium-restricted diet. If you read the labels and note the number of sodium additives in the products, you will understand why they will have to be eliminated for the duration of the doctor's orders. The average soup can or package has over 2000 milligrams of sodium, and often much more.

Instead, here are a group of salt-free soups that have good flavor. If desired, follow the recipe for the whole family, remove the patient's portion, and season the rest according to your taste. It is a good idea to make a quantity of chicken broth or turkey stock without salt and freeze it in ice-cube trays. Then remove from the trays and store in plastic bags in the freezer. Two cubes will provide a small portion of soup. Or, for quick flavorful soups, melt the cubes and add them to low-sodium canned vegetables in an electric blender.

All the soups in this chapter may be frozen in plastic containers for future use. It's well worth the effort because there is no better way to say "I care" than by serving homemade soup.

*This recipe may be used for all low-sodium diets, but those restricted to 1000-, 500-, or 250-mg. low-sodium diets should not eat the carrots or celery used for flavoring.*

# Chicken Soup

1 stewing chicken, about 4 pounds
2 quarts water
2 peeled onions
4 scraped carrots
4 celery stalks with the tops
1 parsnip, cleaned (optional)
2 sprigs parsley
4 stems dillweed
¼ teaspoon white pepper
2 teaspoons sugar

Clean and wash the chicken. Place in a deep pot and cover with water. Add onions, carrots, celery, parsnip, parsley, dillweed, white pepper, and sugar. Bring to a boil, then lower heat, cover, and simmer until chicken is tender (approximately two hours). Remove chicken, strain soup, and chill. Remove any fat that rises to the top of the chilled soup. Reheat soup, adding additional white pepper and sugar according to taste. Serve with a piece of soup carrot and pieces of chicken in each bowl, if desired.

*Makes 8 servings.*

*This recipe may be prepared for all low-sodium diets, but those restricted to 1000-, 500-, or 250-mg. low-sodium diets should omit the spinach.*

# Egg Drop Soup

**1 quart salt-free chicken broth (see index)**
**8 fresh spinach leaves**
**1 egg**

Pour chicken broth into a medium saucepan. Trim and wash fresh spinach leaves. Add to the chicken broth and simmer until limp (about 10 minutes). Beat the egg. Bring the broth to a rolling boil; pour a steady stream of beaten egg into the boiling soup, stirring constantly, as strands of cooked egg are formed. Serve a spinach leaf in each portion.

*Makes 6 to 8 cup-size servings.*

*This recipe may be prepared for all low-sodium diets, but those restricted to 1000-, 500-, or 250-mg. low-sodium diets should omit the sprinkling of Parmesan cheese and the addition of Worcestershire sauce.*

# Onion Soup

**1 quart salt-free chicken broth (see index)**
**4 large onions, thinly sliced**
**1 tablespoon unsalted butter or margarine**
**¼ teaspoon Worcestershire sauce**
**2 tablespoons grated fresh Parmesan cheese**

Pour chicken broth into a large saucepan. Sauté onions in butter until limp and translucent; add to the chicken broth. Add Worcestershire sauce and simmer, covered, for 20 minutes. Serve topped with a sprinkling of Parmesan cheese.

*Makes 6 to 8 servings.*

# Turkey Stock

**1 turkey carcass, about 3 pounds**
**6 cups water**
**1 celery stalk with leaves, cut up**
**1 peeled and thickly sliced onion**
**1 peeled carrot**
**3 sprigs parsley**
**1 crushed bay leaf**
**3 cloves**
**¼ teaspoon ground pepper**

Break up turkey carcass and place in a large saucepan. Add water, celery, onion, carrot, parsley, bay leaf, cloves, and pepper. Cover and bring to boil. Reduce the heat and simmer 3 to 4 hours, stirring occasionally. Strain the stock, remove the meat from the bones, and return the meat to the stock. If necessary, add sufficient water to make 4 cups. Chill. Remove any fat that rises to the top of the chilled stock.

Freeze in ½ cup portions or in ice-cube trays. Remove frozen stock cubes and store in a plastic freezer bag for easy accessibility.

*Makes 4 cups.*

*This recipe may be prepared for all low-sodium diets, but those restricted to 500- or 250-mg. low-sodium diets should substitute low-sodium milk for regular milk.*

## Turkey-Mushroom Soup

3 tablespoons unsalted butter or margarine
½ cup finely chopped fresh mushrooms
3 tablespoons flour
2 cups milk
1 cup turkey stock with meat (see index)
1 teaspoon grated lemon rind

Melt butter in a saucepan. Sauté mushrooms in butter for about 2 minutes. Stir in flour. Remove from heat and gradually stir in milk and turkey stock. Cook over medium heat, stirring constantly, until thickened. Cook an additional 2 minutes. Stir in lemon rind. Serve at once.

*Makes 4 servings.*

*This recipe may be prepared for all low-sodium diets; but those restricted to 1000-, 500-, or 250-mg. low-sodium diets should not eat the carrots and celery used for flavoring.*

# Vegetable Soup

**4 beef marrow bones**
**2 quarts water**
**2 sliced onions**
**½ cup barley**
**2 peeled and sliced carrots**
**3 tomatoes, cut up**
**1 large potato, peeled and cut up**
**2 sliced celery stalks**
**½ pound trimmed green beans, cut up**
**½ pound shelled peas**
**1 bay leaf**
**½ teaspoon sugar**
**¼ teaspoon pepper**
**2 tablespoons farina (optional)**

Place beef bones in a large pot and cover with water. Add sliced onions and barley. Bring to a boil, then turn down heat and simmer for about 30 minutes, occasionally skimming residue off the top. Add the rest of the ingredients, cover, and cook for 30 minutes more, or until all vegetables are tender. If a thicker soup is desired, add farina at this point and stir until cooked through.

*Makes 8 servings.*

*This recipe may be prepared for all low-sodium diets, but those restricted to 1000-, 500-, or 250-mg. low-sodium diets should not eat the carrots and celery used for flavoring and should omit the Parmesan cheese.*

# Minestrone Soup

4 beef marrow bones
2 sliced onions
2 cups shredded cabbage
3 peeled and diced potatoes
2 diced celery stalks
2 scraped and diced carrots
½ cup raw rice
2 quarts water
1 minced garlic clove
3 minced parsley sprigs
1 teaspoon dried basil
¼ teaspoon pepper
1 bay leaf
1 cup cooked kidney beans
¼ cup grated Parmesan cheese

Place marrow bones in a heavy pot. Add onions, cabbage, potatoes, celery, carrots, and rice. Cover with water. Add garlic, parsley, basil, pepper, and bay leaf. Bring to a boil, then reduce heat and simmer, covered, for about 1 hour. Skim residue off the top occasionally. Add cooked kidney beans. Garnish with grated Parmesan cheese sprinkled over each serving.

*Makes 8 to 10 servings.*

*This recipe may be prepared for all low-sodium diets, but those restricted to 1000-, 500-, or 250-mg. should omit using a carrot in the preparation of this soup. Those restricted to 500- or 250-mg. should substitute low-sodium milk for regular milk.*

## Mushroom-Barley Soup

2 beef marrow bones
¾ pound sliced fresh mushrooms
⅓ cup barley
1 diced onion
1 scraped and finely diced carrot
1½ quarts water
2 finely chopped sprigs dillweed
2 finely chopped sprigs parsley
¼ teaspoon pepper
3 tablespoons farina
1 cup milk

Place bones, mushrooms, barley, onion, and carrot into a deep pot. Add water, dillweed, parsley, and pepper. Bring to a boil, then reduce heat and cover; simmer for one hour. Stir farina into milk and add to the soup, stirring constantly. Let soup thicken and then serve.

*Makes 8 servings.*

## Gazpacho

4 large tomatoes, cut up
1 peeled garlic clove
2 tablespoons olive oil
1 egg
¼ cup dry sherry
2 tablespoons wine vinegar
¼ teaspoon pepper
1 teaspoon sugar

1 peeled and diced cucumber
1 seeded and diced green pepper
3 finely sliced scallions

Cream tomatoes in an electric blender, a few pieces at a time, until smooth. Pour half into a separate container. Add garlic, olive oil, egg, sherry, vinegar, pepper, and sugar to the half remaining in the blender. Process again until smooth. Pour into the tomato container and stir together. Refrigerate until well chilled. Serve in small chilled bowls. At the table, pass bowls of cucumber, green pepper, and scallions to be used as garnishes for the soup.

*Makes 4 servings.*

*This recipe may be prepared for all low-sodium diets, but those restricted to 500- or 250-mg. low-sodium diets should substitute low-sodium milk for regular milk.*

## Fish Chowder

2 peeled and cubed potatoes
2 thinly sliced onions
1 finely chopped dillweed sprig
2 cups water
1 pound fish fillets
2 cups milk
2 tablespoons unsalted butter or margarine
¼ teaspoon thyme
¼ teaspoon white pepper

Simmer potatoes, onions, and dillweed in water, covered, until potatoes are soft (approximately 15 minutes). Cut fish fillets into small chunks and add to the potatoes. Stir in the milk, butter, thyme, and pepper. Simmer, covered, for an additional 15 to 20 minutes, stirring occasionally. Serve at once.

*Makes 6 servings.*

# Cabbage Soup

4 meaty beef neck bones
2 quarts water
2 sliced onions
1 medium-sized cabbage, thinly sliced
4 large tomatoes, cut up
2 peeled and diced potatoes
2 bay leaves
¼ cup white seedless raisins
¼ cup lemon juice
2 tablespoons brown sugar
½ teaspoon pepper

Place meat bones and water in a large deep pot; bring to a boil. Skim surface with a large spoon to remove residue. Then add onions, cabbage, tomatoes, potatoes, bay leaves, raisins, lemon juice, brown sugar, and pepper. Simmer for 2 to 3 hours. Add more lemon juice or sugar to obtain the desired balance of the sweet and sour taste. Remove bones, scrape off the meat, and return meat to soup.

*Makes 8 servings.*

*This recipe may be used for all low-sodium diets, but those restricted to 500- or 250-mg. low-sodium diets should substitute low-sodium milk for regular milk.*

# Potato-Leek Soup

4 large potatoes, peeled and cut up
1 large sliced leek
2 cups water
1 finely chopped parsley sprig
¼ teaspoon white pepper
4 cups hot milk
1 large sliced onion

2 tablespoons unsalted butter or margarine
2 tablespoons flour
  Chopped chives (optional)
  Paprika (optional)

Place the potatoes and leek in a saucepan. Add water, parsley, and pepper. Cover and cook over low heat until potatoes are tender. Mash potatoes and leek in the potato water. Add hot milk. Sauté sliced onion in butter until soft and translucent. Quickly blend in flour and several tablespoons of the hot potato mixture; stir until smooth. Then stir the onion mixture into the potato mixture; heat and stir until smooth. Serve garnished with a sprinkling of chopped chives and a dash of paprika, if desired.

*Makes 8 servings.*

## Tomato-Rice Soup

6 fresh tomatoes
3 beef marrow bones
1½ quarts water
2 finely diced onions
2 tablespoons sugar
½ teaspoon paprika
¼ teaspoon pepper
¼ teaspoon dried basil
  Juice of 1 lemon
3 tablespoons cream of rice cereal
1 cup cooked rice

Briefly dip tomatoes into boiling water and peel them. Cut them up and place in a deep pot. Add marrow bones, water, onions, sugar, paprika, pepper, basil, and the juice of 1 lemon. Simmer for about 2 hours, covered. Stir some of the hot soup into the cream of rice until smooth, then add this mixture to the soup, stirring as it thickens. Add cooked rice and heat through.

*Makes 6 to 8 servings.*

*This recipe may be used for all low-sodium diets, but those restricted to 500- or 250-mg. low-sodium diets should substitute milk for regular milk.*

# Split Pea Soup

**2 cups split peas**
**4 meaty beef neck bones**
**2 quarts water**
**2 finely diced onions**
**2 finely diced parsley sprigs**
**2 finely diced dillweed sprigs**
**1 bay leaf**
**1 teaspoon sugar**
**¼ teaspoon pepper**
**2 tablespoons cream of rice cereal**
**¼ cup milk**

Rinse and soak split peas for several hours or overnight. Place in a deep pot with the neck bones and water. Add onions, parsley, dillweed, bay leaf, sugar, and pepper. Bring to a boil, then reduce heat and simmer for about 2 hours, stirring occasionally. Skim residue off the surface of the soup as it rises to the top. Remove the meat and the bones. Pour the soup through a sieve or a food mill, forcing through the vegetables. Return the soup to the pot. Mix the cream of rice with the milk and add to the soup. Heat and stir constantly until soup thickens. Serve with cut-up pieces of cooked neck meat, if desired.

*Makes 8 servings.*

*This recipe may be prepared for all low-sodium diets. Those restricted to 500- or 250-mg. low-sodium diets should substitute low-sodium milk for regular milk and omit the croutons. Those on 1000-mg. low-sodium diets should omit the croutons also.*

# Lentil Soup

1 cup dried lentils
1 quart water
2 cups milk
1 tablespoon unsalted butter or margarine
1 tablespoon flour
1 teaspoon paprika
1 teaspoon sugar
  Croutons

Pick over and wash the lentils. Soak them in water for about 3 hours, or overnight. Drain; bring 1 quart water to a boil and add lentils. Cook over very low heat until soft and the water is reduced to half its volume. Mash the liquid and lentils through a sieve or food mill and return to the cooking pot. Stir in the milk and bring to a boil. Meanwhile, melt the butter in a small saucepan and stir in the flour; cook for a few moments, stirring constantly. Add the flour mixture to the soup by spooning some of the soup first into the flour mixture until smooth and then stirring it all back into the soup pot. Add paprika and sugar. Serve with croutons.

*Makes 6 servings.*

*This recipe may be prepared for all low-sodium diets, but those restricted to 500- or 250-mg. low-sodium diets should substitute low-sodium milk for the light cream.*

# Broccoli Bisque

**1 package (10 ounces) frozen chopped broccoli**
**1 small sliced onion**
**2 cups salt-free chicken broth (see index)**
**1 whole clove**
**⅛ teaspoon pepper**
**1 cup light cream**
**1 tablespoon dry sherry**

Place broccoli, onion, and chicken broth in a medium-sized saucepan. Add clove and pepper. Cover and cook until broccoli is soft. Remove clove. In an electric blender or a food mill process the ingredients until smooth. Pour back into the saucepan, stir in the light cream, and heat through. Stir in the sherry and serve at once.

*Makes 6 servings.*

*This recipe may be prepared for all low-sodium diets, but those restricted to 500- or 250-mg. low-sodium diets should substitute low-sodium milk for the light cream.*

# Cream of Pumpkin Soup

2 cups cooked mashed pumpkin
1 small onion, finely diced
1 tablespoon unsalted butter or margarine
1 quart salt-free chicken broth (see index)
2 tablespoons cornstarch
¼ teaspoon ground ginger
¼ teaspoon ground nutmeg
1 cup light cream
1 egg
  Popcorn (optional)

Place cooked mashed pumpkin in a heavy saucepan. Sauté onion in butter until golden; add to pumpkin. Stir in the chicken broth and cook over low heat. In a separate bowl stir cornstarch, ginger, and nutmeg into light cream; beat an egg into this mixture. Pour cream mixture into pumpkin mixture and cook over low heat until thickened (approximately 5 minutes), stirring constantly. Serve hot, garnished with unsalted popcorn if desired.

*Makes 8 servings.*

# 6

# Salt-Free Eggs

Y OU won't have to worry about tasteless eggs if you follow the recipes that make this high protein food a pleasure to eat.

A good rule of thumb is to limit your intake of eggs to one a day, including those used in cooking and baking. This is due to the relatively high natural sodium content of egg whites and to the much debated high cholesterol count of egg yolks.

It is possible that the same reason that places you on a sodium-restricted regime also is reason to limit your intake of eggs to less than one a day. Many doctors prescribe only three eggs a week, but it is important to question whether this is in addition to those used in baking. Only then can you begin a successful menu planning program.

When ordering eggs in a restaurant, be sure to specify that poached eggs be prepared without the addition of salt to the water or the egg. Insist that fried eggs be prepared in a skillet with sweet butter rather than on the griddle that is used for bacon and ham. Choose a jelly omelet over a cheese or Spanish omelet, and when in doubt choose boiled eggs to be brought to you in the shell.

*This recipe may be prepared for all low-sodium diets, but those restricted to 500- or 250-mg. low-sodium diets should substitute low-sodium milk for the light cream.*

# Shirred Eggs

**6 eggs**
**2 tablespoons unsalted butter or margarine**
**2 tablespoons light cream**
  **Dash of white pepper**

Preheat oven to 400° F. Grease well a shallow baking dish and break the eggs, one at a time, into it, making sure that the yolks remain whole. Melt the butter and remove from heat. Stir in cream and pepper. Drizzle the butter-cream mixture over the eggs. Bake about 20 minutes or until set. Serve at once.

*Makes 6 servings.*

# Scrambled Eggs and Corn

**2 cooked ears of corn**
**2 tablespoons unsalted butter or margarine**
**4 eggs**
  **Dash of pepper**
**⅛ teaspoon dried tarragon**

Cut corn from the cobs. Melt butter in a large skillet and add corn. Beat the eggs together and pour over corn. Sprinkle with pepper and tarragon. As the mixture cooks push it towards the center of the skillet to permit liquid mixture to run towards the edge. Serve as soon as the eggs are set.

*Makes 2 or 3 servings.*

## Cottage Cheese Scramble

**4 eggs**
  **Dash of white pepper**
**1 tablespoon chopped chives**
**1 tablespoon unsalted butter or margarine**
**½ cup low-sodium cottage cheese**

Break eggs into a bowl and beat with a fork or whisk; add pepper and chives. Heat butter in a large skillet. Pour in the egg mixture and reduce the heat enough to cook the eggs quickly. Lift the mixture from the bottom and sides as it thickens. As the cooked mixture is lifted the thin uncooked part should flow to the bottom. Avoid constant stirring. When eggs are almost thickened throughout, stir cottage cheese into the egg mixture. The cottage cheese will melt and coat the eggs. Remove from the heat as soon as the cottage cheese is melted and serve at once.

*Makes 2 to 4 servings.*

*This recipe may be used for all low-sodium diets, but those restricted to 500- or 250-mg. low-sodium diets should substitute low-sodium milk for regular milk.*

## Puffed Jelly Omelet

4 eggs, separated
1 tablespoon milk
1 tablespoon unsalted butter or margarine
¼ cup jelly, any flavor
1 teaspoon confectioners' sugar

Beat the egg whites until stiff peaks form. In a separate bowl beat the egg yolks and milk together. Fold gently into the beaten egg whites until thoroughly combined. Melt butter in a large skillet and pour in the egg mixture. Cook until lightly browned and solidified. Spread jelly over half the omelet and cover the jelly-spread half with other half of the omelet. Sprinkle with confectioners' sugar.

*Makes 2 to 3 servings.*

*This recipe may be used for all low-sodium diets, but those restricted to 500- or 250-mg. low-sodium diets should substitute low-sodium milk for regular milk.*

## Tomato-Pepper Omelet

2 tablespoons unsalted butter or margarine
1 diced onion
1 diced green pepper
1 diced tomato
4 eggs
2 tablespoons milk

Melt butter in a skillet; add onion, green pepper, and tomato. Stir and cook for several minutes or until onion is translucent. Beat eggs and milk together; pour over vegetables in the skillet. Push mixture towards the center of the skillet as it solidifies, letting the liquid egg run to the edge. Fold over and serve.

*Makes 2 to 3 servings.*

## Strawberry Omelet

**1 cup fresh strawberries**
**2 tablespoons sugar**
**4 eggs**
**¼ cup water**
**1 tablespoon unsalted butter or margarine**
**1 teaspoon confectioners' sugar**

Wash and hull the strawberries and sprinkle with sugar. Place in a container and cover tightly. Place in refrigerator for at least four hours, or, preferably, overnight. Shake the container occasionally to distribute sugar. This will produce slightly soft and sweetened strawberries with some natural juice.

To make the omelet beat eggs and water together. Melt the butter in a large skillet. Pour in the egg mixture. As the egg sets at the edge, carefully draw the cooked portions toward the center, allowing the uncooked portions to flow to the bottom. Slide pan rapidly back and forth over the heat to keep mixture in motion and sliding freely. Keep mixture as level as possible. When the eggs are set and the surface is still moist, remove the pan from the heat and slip onto a serving plate. Spoon strawberries onto half of the omelet and fold the other half over the strawberries. Sprinkle with confectioners' sugar.

*Makes 2 servings.*

# Poached Eggs

2 eggs
1 teaspoon vinegar
2 sliced low-sodium toast or toasted
  low-sodium English muffins

For easier poaching, eggs should be kept cold until the last moment. Fill a skillet with water and bring to a bubbling boil; add vinegar. Stir the water in a circular motion and break an egg into the center of the circle; repeat. Reduce heat. Push spreading egg whites back over the yolks with a spoon until they solidify. Cook for about 4 minutes. Remove eggs with a slotted spoon and serve on toast.

*Makes 2 servings.*

*This recipe may be used for mild sodium-restricted diets only. Those restricted to 1000-, 500-, or 250-mg. low-sodium diets should omit this recipe.*

# Eggs Florentine

1 package (10 ounces) frozen chopped spinach
2 tablespoons unsalted butter or margarine
4 eggs

Preheat oven to 350° F. Cook spinach according to directions on the package; drain well. Mix butter into the spinach until melted. Grease 4 individual baking dishes with unsalted butter or margarine. Spoon the spinach into the baking dishes. In the center of each make a depression large enough to hold one raw egg. Break an egg into each center. Bake for 10 to 15 minutes or until egg is firm to your taste.

*Makes 4 servings.*

*This recipe may be prepared for all low-sodium diets, but those restricted to 1000-, 500-, or 250-mg. low-sodium diets should substitute low-sodium bread for regular bread and omit the Parmesan cheese.*

# Chive, Mushroom and Egg Casserole

3 slices white bread
6 tablespoons unsalted butter or margarine
2 tablespoons chopped chives
½ pound sliced mushrooms
6 eggs
⅛ teaspoon pepper
3 tablespoons grated Parmesan cheese

Preheat oven to 350° F. Cut bread slices into halves diagonally. Heat 2 tablespoons butter in a skillet and brown bread slices on both sides until golden. Grease well a shallow casserole with unsalted butter or margarine and place bread in the bottom of it. Heat 2 tablespoons butter in the skillet and sauté chives and mushrooms until tender. Drop eggs, side by side, into the lined casserole. Spoon the mushroom mixture around the edge of the casserole. Sprinkle with pepper. Sprinkle Parmesan cheese over the mushroom mixture. Dot top of eggs with 2 tablespoons butter. Bake for 30 to 35 minutes or until eggs are set.

*Makes 6 servings.*

*This recipe may be prepared for all low-sodium diets, but those restricted to 1000-, 500-, or 250-mg. low-sodium diets should substitute blender mayonnaise (see index).*

# Deviled Eggs

6 peeled hard-boiled eggs
1 tablespoon dairy sour cream
⅛ teaspoon dry mustard
⅛ teaspoon pepper
⅛ teaspoon paprika

Cut eggs in half lengthwise. Scoop out the yolks and place in a bowl, reserving the whites. Mash the yolks; add sour cream, dry mustard, and pepper, mixing well. Spoon mixture back into the reserved whites, mounding the yolks carefully in their cavities. Sprinkle paprika over the yolks. Chill until ready to serve.

*Makes 12 deviled eggs.*

# Egg and Macaroni Salad

2 cups elbow macaroni
3 quarts boiling water
1 cucumber
½ cup chopped red onion
¼ teaspoon dillweed
⅛ teaspoon pepper
3 tablespoons tarragon vinegar
2 tablespoons salad oil
8 hard-boiled eggs
⅔ cup blender mayonnaise (see index)
  Lettuce

Cook macaroni in boiling water, stirring occasionally, until tender. Drain in a colander, rinse with cold water and drain again. Dice ¾ of the cucumber; slice the remainder of the cucumber and reserve for garnish. Mix together the macaroni, diced cucumber, onion, dillweed, pepper, vinegar, and salad oil and chill. Coarsely chop 6 of the eggs; slice the remaining 2 eggs. Add the chopped eggs and mayonnaise to the macaroni mixture and mix lightly. Arrange salad in a bowl lined with lettuce leaves and garnish with the sliced eggs and cucumbers.

*Makes 6 servings.*

 *This recipe may be prepared for all low-sodium diets, but those restricted to 500- or 250-mg. low-sodium diets should substitute low-sodium bread for regular bread and low-sodium milk for regular milk.*

# Creamed Eggs on Toast

6 hard-boiled eggs
2 tablespoons unsalted butter or margarine
2 tablespoons flour
2 cups milk
½ teaspoon chopped dillweed
⅛ teaspoon white pepper
4 slices of toast
2 tablespoons chopped parsley
¼ teaspoon paprika

Slice eggs into thin rounds. Melt butter in a saucepan; stir in flour and then gradually stir in milk. Cook, stirring constantly, until smooth and thickened. Add dillweed, pepper, and sliced eggs. Heat through and spoon over toast slices. Sprinkle with parsley and paprika. Serve at once.

*Makes 4 servings.*

# 7

# Salt-Free Meats

CULINARY skills are really challenged by salt-free diet limitations. Knowledge of the subtle uses of herbs and spices eases the monotony of putting the saltshaker away. Many recipes call for a combination of herbs, onions, and garlic to heighten flavor. You may become fond of this combination and other combinations found in these recipes and will soon discover that they may be substituted in your own favorite recipes. Just remember that a little bit of herbs and spices goes a long way to please the palate, and too much can ruin a good thing.

Do not serve brains or kidneys to the low-sodium restricted patient. Omit canned, salted, or smoked meats, including bacon, ham, bologna, chipped beef, luncheon meats, frankfurters, sausages, smoked tongue, and corned beef. Meats koshered with salt are also to be eliminated. All other fresh meats may be used according to the doctor's instructions.

Figure that each ounce of cooked meat has 25 milligrams of natural sodium in it. In order to produce a three-ounce portion of cooked meat, you will have to start with four ounces of boneless raw meat or five to six ounces of meat with fat and bone attached.

If one is on a low-cholesterol diet as well, trim all fat from the meat before eating. Limit the patient to three beef meals a week and select recipes for veal, chicken, or fish for the rest of the week's menus.

Above all, keep meals interesting and delicious, using a

tempting variety of dishes to help the low-sodium dieter forget the deprivation of salt. Use salt substitutes only after discussing it with the doctor, because many contain ingredients that may also be restricted. A little pepper may perk up flavors but alone it can become a boring substitute. The patient can discover that it is not necessary to forego the pleasure of dining just because there is a sodium restriction.

Wine has been used freely to give flair to many of these recipes, but do not use the "cooking wines" sold in regular food markets. These wines have sodium added to prevent them from being used as alcoholic beverages, and are in no way as satisfactory as regular inexpensive table wines made from pure grapes. If you choose a good wine with a screw-on cap for cooking— burgundy and/or sauterne—you can keep it in the regrigerator without worrying about the wine spoiling because of a damaged cork. Don't worry about the calories when cooking with wine—they evaporate while the flavor remains.

*This recipe may be used for all sodium-restricted diets. Those restricted to 1000-, 500-, or 250-mg. low-sodium diets should substitute low-sodium bread crumbs for regular bread crumbs and omit the Parmesan cheese.*

## Meat Loaf

2 pounds lean ground beef
1 grated small onion
1 egg
½ cup unseasoned bread crumbs
¼ cup chopped parsley
2 tablespoons grated Parmesan cheese

¼ teaspoon pepper
⅛ teaspoon cinnamon

Preheat oven to 350° F. Combine all ingredients, mixing well. Pack into a loaf pan. Bake for 1 hour.

*Makes 6 to 8 servings.*

*This recipe may be used for all sodium-restricted diets. Those restricted to 500- or 250-mg. low-sodium diets should substitute low-sodium milk for regular milk.*

## Spicy Meat Loaf

2 pounds ground beef
2 eggs, lightly beaten
2 slices low-sodium bread, crumbled
½ cup milk
1 small onion, grated
1 teaspoon crushed coriander seed
¼ teaspoon pepper
⅛ teaspoon allspice

Preheat oven to 350° F. Combine ground beef and beaten eggs. Soak crumbled bread in milk and add to mixture. Add onion, coriander seed, pepper, and allspice; mix well. Place in a 9-by-5-by-3-inch loaf pan. Bake for 1 hour and 15 minutes.

*Makes 8 servings.*

# Herb Burgers

1 pound ground beef
¼ teaspoon pepper
1 tablespoon minced onion
¼ teaspoon marjoram
⅛ teaspoon thyme
1 tablespoon chopped parsley

Combine ground beef, pepper, minced onion, marjoram, thyme, and chopped parsley. Shape into patties. Cook on a grill, broil, or fry.

*Makes 4 servings.*

# Pineapple Glazed Hamburgers

1 pound lean ground beef
4 canned pineapple rings
2 teaspoons brown sugar

Form ground beef into four hamburger patties. Broil for 5 minutes. Turn and place a pineapple ring on top of each hamburger; sprinkle the pineapple with brown sugar. Broil again for 5 minutes or until done to your taste. Serve at once.

*Makes 4 servings.*

# Surprise Burgers

1 pound ground beef
1 tablespoon grated onion
2 tablespoons chopped parsley
¼ teaspoon pepper
4 thin slices tomato
4 thin slices onion

Break up meat in a mixing bowl and work in the grated onion, parsley, and pepper. Shape into 8 thin patties. Top 4 of the patties with a slice of tomato and a slice of onion; cover with remaining patties and press edges together to seal. Broil for 3 to 4 minutes on each side or until done to your taste.

*Makes 4 servings.*

*This recipe may be used for all sodium-restricted diets. Those restricted to 1000-, 500-, or 250-mg. low-sodium diets should substitute low-sodium bread crumbs for regular bread crumbs.*

## Meatballs in Cranberry Sauce

**1 pound lean ground beef**
**1 egg**
**⅓ cup unseasoned bread crumbs**
**⅛ teaspoon pepper**
**¼ teaspoon oregano**
**2 tomatoes**
**½ cup low-sodium cranberry sauce**
  **Juice of ½ lemon**
  **Cooking oil**

Combine ground beef with egg, bread crumbs, pepper, and oregano. Place the tomatoes in an electric blender and purée. Add cranberry sauce and lemon juice to the tomato purée and blend together. Form ground beef mixture into tiny meatballs. In a heavy skillet brown the meatballs in oil. Pour off the excess oil and add the tomato-cranberry sauce to the meatballs. Cover and simmer for 45 minutes.

*Makes 4 servings.*

*This recipe may be used for all low sodium-restricted diets. Those restricted to 1000-, 500-, or 250-mg. low-sodium diets should omit the celery.*

# Beef and Noodles

2 coarsely chopped tomatoes
½ cup water
1½ teaspoon oregano
¼ teaspoon thyme
¼ teaspoon pepper
3 tablespoons salad oil
1 pound ground beef
1 cup chopped onions
1 crushed garlic clove
1 diced green pepper
1 cup sliced celery
½ cup chopped parsley
8 ounces cooked broad noodles

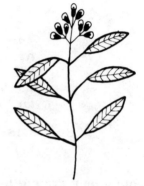

Combine tomatoes, water, oregano, thyme, and pepper; set aside. Heat oil in a heavy skillet; add meat and stir constantly until browned. Remove meat with a slotted spoon and set aside. Sauté onion, garlic, green pepper, and celery in the drippings in the skillet until tender. Cover the skillet and cook mixture about 7 minutes over low heat, stirring occasionally. Stir in parsley. Add the meat, the tomato mixture, and the hot cooked noodles to the skillet and lightly toss. Cook for a few minutes until heated through.

*Makes 4 servings.*

*This recipe may be used for all sodium-restricted diets. Those restricted to 1000-, 500-, or 250-mg. low-sodium diets should substitute low-sodium bread crumbs for regular bread crumbs.*

## Stuffed Beef Rolls

1½ pounds beef top round
¼ cup chopped onion
¼ cup unsalted butter or margarine
2 cups soft bread crumbs
2 cups applesauce
¼ teaspoon thyme
¼ cup olive oil
1 cup sliced onion
½ cup apple juice or water
⅛ teaspoon ginger

Have butcher cut beef in slices about 3-by-4 inches. Pound each slice until thin with a meat mallet. Sauté chopped onion in butter until tender. Add bread crumbs, ½ cup applesauce, and thyme. Mix thoroughly. Spread a little applesauce filling on each meat slice. Roll up like a jelly roll and tie each with a string. Brown meat rolls in oil and remove from skillet. (There should be about 2 tablespoons of oil left in the pan.) Add sliced onion and and cook until golden brown. Add remaining 1½ cups applesauce and apple juice; mix well. Add ginger. Place meat rolls in sauce. Cover and simmer 1 hour or until meat is tender, adding more apple juice as the liquid cooks away.

*Makes 6 servings.*

# Fillet of Beef in Wine

1 4-pound fillet of beef
½ teaspoon paprika
2 tablespoons finely chopped onion
1 cup dry red wine
½ cup boiling water

Preheat oven to 450° F. Place fillet of beef in an open roasting pan. Sprinkle with paprika. Rub all over with onion, adding excess onion to the roasting pan. Pour red wine over the fillet and let stand for 20 minutes; then turn and let stand for 20 minutes more. Turn right side up and place in the oven; cook 25 minutes for rare meat or 30 minutes for medium rare. Remove from the oven and place on a warm platter. Pour ¼ to ½ cup boiling water into the roasting pan, scraping and stirring the wine and drippings until a thin gravy is formed; serve with meat. To carve the meat, angle the knife slightly to get broader slices.

*Serves 8 to 10.*

*This recipe may be used for all mild sodium-restricted diets, but those restricted to 1000-, 500-, or 250-mg. low-sodium diets should omit the carrots and celery from the recipe or refrain from eating the gravy.*

## Swiss Steak

3 pounds round steak, cut 1½ inches thick
1 finely chopped garlic clove
¼ cup flour
¼ teaspoon paprika
⅛ teaspoon pepper
3 tablespoons cooking oil
1 sliced onion
¼ cup thinly sliced celery
½ cup thinly sliced carrots
1 finely chopped dill sprig
2 coarsely chopped tomatoes
  Boiling water

Rub round steak with chopped garlic on both sides. Combine flour, paprika, and pepper; pound this mixture into the surface of the meat, using a meat mallet or heavy saucer. Heat oil in a heavy skillet and sauté onion until translucent; push aside. Brown meat in the skillet, turning to sear all sides. Lower heat and add celery, carrots, dill, and chopped tomatoes. Add a little water. Cover and cook over low heat for 2 to 3 hours or until tender, adding additional boiling water if needed.

*Makes 6 to 8 servings.*

# Boiled Beef

3 pounds beef chuck or round
¼ teaspoon pepper
1 tablespoon salad oil
2 cups boiling water
1 sliced onion
2 bay leaves
¼ teaspoon dry mustard

Lightly dust the beef with pepper. Heat oil in a heavy pot. Brown on all sides, searing in the natural juices. Pour in boiling water; add onion and bay leaves. Cover tightly and simmer over low heat for 2½ to 3 hours or until fork tender. Remove meat from liquid; turn heat high and reduce the remaining liquid to half its volume. Add mustard to the reduced gravy and serve with the boiled beef.

*Makes 6 to 8 servings.*

# Brisket Pot Roast

4-pound brisket of beef, preferably a lean first cut
2 sliced onions
1 cup water
2 bay leaves
¼ teaspoon pepper
¼ teaspoon paprika

Preheat oven to 325° F. Arrange brisket in a Dutch oven or covered baking pan. Cover with sliced onions. Pour water around beef and add bay leaves to the water. Sprinkle pepper and paprika over top of the beef. Cover and roast for about 3 hours or until tender.

*Makes 6 to 8 servings.*

# Sauerbraten

**4 pound beef top round roast**
**⅛ teaspoon pepper**
**½ garlic clove**
**2 cups red wine vinegar**
**1 cup water**
**¼ cup sugar**
**1 chopped onion**
**2 bay leaves**
**½ teaspoon ground ginger**
**6 whole peppercorns**
**¼ cup flour**
**¼ cup olive oil**

Sprinkle beef roast with pepper and rub on all sides with the cut side of garlic clove. Place roast on end in a large plastic bag and set in a deep bowl. Heat wine vinegar, water, sugar, onion, bay leaves, ginger, and peppercorns together in a saucepan; simmer for about 5 minutes. Cool slightly and pour into plastic bag over the roast; fasten the bag with a wire tie. Refrigerate for a day or two, turning the bag occasionally to redistribute the marinade. When ready to cook, remove the meat and wipe dry. Pat meat with flour. Heat oil in a Dutch oven; brown meat on all sides over high heat, searing the juices in. Reduce heat and add the remaining marinade. Simmer, covered, for 2 hours or until meat is tender. Serve in thick slices with gravy.

*Makes 6 to 8 servings.*

*This recipe may be prepared for all low-sodium diets, but those restricted to 1000-, 500-, or 250-mg. low-sodium diets should not eat the carrots and celery used for flavoring.*

# Beef Stew Au Vin

2 pounds lean cubed beef
3 large tomatoes, cut in small wedges
4 carrots, cut in 1-inch slices
4 stalks celery, cut in 1-inch slices
2 thinly sliced onions
2 green peppers, seeded and cut up
6 potatoes, pared and cut up
½ cup burgundy wine
½ cup water
2 bay leaves
¼ teaspoon pepper
¼ teaspoon dried basil

Preheat oven to 350° F. Combine all ingredients in a Dutch oven or large ovenproof pan with a tight-fitting lid. Cover and place in the oven. Cook for 1½ hours or until meat is fork tender.

*Makes 6 to 8 servings.*

## Curried Beef Stew

2 tablespoons unsalted butter or margarine
1 pound beef stew meat, cut in chunks
2 cups low-sodium canned tomatoes
1 tablespoon chili powder
1 teaspoon curry powder
12 small whole white onions
2 cups canned low-sodium green beans

Melt butter in a heavy saucepan; sauté beef chunks, until nicely browned. Add tomatoes, chili powder, curry powder, and onions. Cover and simmer until beef is tender (approximately 1 to 1½ hours). Add green beans. Continue to simmer until heated through.

*Makes 6 servings.*

## London Broil

½ finely diced small onion
½ minced garlic clove
¼ teaspoon black pepper
2 tablespoons salad oil
2 pounds flank steak

Combine onion, garlic, pepper, and oil; rub over both sides of flank steak. Place in a broiling pan and set in refrigerator for ½ hour, absorbing the flavors. Broil steak for about 5 minutes on each side. Carve meat on an extreme diagonal across the grain into thin slices. Serve at once.

*Makes 4 to 6 servings.*

# Steak Au Poivre

4 boneless rib steaks, 8 ounces each
  Freshly ground pepper
4 teaspoons unsalted butter or margarine, melted
  A few drops of Tabasco sauce
¼ cup lemon juice
¼ cup cognac (optional)
1 tablespoon chopped parsley
1 tablespoon chopped chives

Sprinkle both sides of each steak with pepper and press into meat with the heel of hand. Place in refrigerator for 30 minutes. Then place on a broiling pan and broil for 3 minutes on each side. Remove to a warm platter. Combine melted butter, Tabasco, and lemon juice; pour over steaks. Heat cognac; ignite and pour over steaks, shaking back and forth until flames die. Serve at once, sprinkled with parsley and chives.

*Serves 4.*

# Rib Roast of Beef

6 pounds rolled or standing rib roast of beef
¼ teaspoon pepper
½ teaspoon paprika
2 tablespoons flour

Preheat oven to 325° F. Wipe meat with a damp cloth or paper towel. Place on a rack in a roasting pan with fat side up. (If using a standing rib roast, stand it on rib bones in a shallow open pan.) Combine pepper, paprika, and flour; pat all over the surface of meat. Roast about 3½ hours for rare meat.

*Makes 10 to 12 servings.*

*This recipe may be used for all sodium-restricted diets, but those restricted to 1000-, 500-, or 250-mg. low-sodium diets should omit the carrots and celery in the recipe or strain the gravy.*

# Shoulder of Veal Roast

**4 or 5 pounds boneless shoulder of veal roast, rolled and tied**
**⅛ teaspoon pepper**
**¼ cup olive oil**
**1 sliced onion**
**1 finely diced garlic clove**
**1 teaspoon dried rosemary**
**¼ cup sliced celery**
**¼ cup sliced carrots**
**2 tomatoes, cut up**
**2 bay leaves**
**2 parsley sprigs**
**1 cup salt-free chicken broth (see index)**
**½ cup dry white wine**

Preheat oven to 350° F. Pat veal roast dry. Sprinkle with pepper. Heat oil in the bottom of a Dutch oven; add onions and garlic and sauté until onions are translucent. Add veal roast and brown on all sides. Remove from heat. Add rosemary, celery, carrots, tomatoes, bay leaves, and parsley. Pour in chicken broth and white wine. Cover and place in the oven for 2 hours, or until fork tender.

*Makes 8 to 10 servings.*

*This recipe may be used for all sodium-restricted diets, but those restricted to 500- or 250-mg. low-sodium diets should omit the light cream.*

# Veal Paprikash

2 pounds thinly sliced veal
2 tablespoons paprika
⅛ teaspoon pepper
3 tablespoons unsalted butter or margarine
3 tomatoes
½ cup water
¾ cup light cream

Sprinkle veal with paprika and pepper. Heat butter in a heavy skillet; brown veal on both sides. Cut up tomatoes and put in an electric blender with ½ cup water; purée and pour this tomato mixture over the veal. Cover and simmer for 35 minutes or until tender. Before serving stir in light cream; heat through but do not bring to a boil. Serve at once.

*Makes 6 servings.*

# Veal Piccata

2 pounds veal scalloppini slices
¼ cup flour
3 tablespoons unsalted butter or margarine
3 tablespoons olive oil
¼ teaspoon pepper
2 lemons
¼ cup chopped fresh parsley

Pound veal slices very thin. Dredge in flour, shaking off excess to leave a fine powdery coating. Heat butter and olive oil in a large heavy skillet; sauté veal slices on both sides. Sprinkle with pepper. Add the juice of 1 lemon. Slice the second lemon very thin and add slices to the skillet. Add chopped parsley. Cook for about 5 minutes, shaking the skillet occasionally. Serve with lemon slices; spoon sauce over veal.

*Makes 6 servings.*

# Herbed Veal

**2 pounds thin veal cutlets**
**3 tablespoons flour**
**2 tablespoons unsalted butter or margarine**
**¼ teaspoon pepper**
**¼ cup nonfat dried milk**
**½ cup water**
**½ teaspoon dried thyme**
**½ teaspoon dried tarragon**

Cut the veal cutlets into serving portions. Cover each slice with waxed paper and pound with the flat side of a cleaver or wooden mallet until ⅛-inch thick. Dredge the cutlets in flour. Heat butter in a large skillet; add cutlets, sprinkle with pepper, and brown lightly on both sides. Remove cutlets to a warm platter. Stir nonfat dried milk into water; add thyme and tarragon and mix until smooth. Stir this mixture into the skillet; heat slowly over low heat, stirring in the brown crusty residue in the pan. Pour sauce over cutlets.

*Makes 6 servings.*

# Veal Balls in Citrus Sauce

VEAL BALLS:

**1½ pounds ground veal**
**1 cup oatmeal**
**2 eggs**
**1 tablespoon brown sugar**
**⅛ teaspoon ground cloves**
**⅛ teaspoon nutmeg**
  **Salad oil**

Combine all ingredients. Shape into 1-inch balls and chill. Lightly brown veal balls in hot salad oil. Drain off excess oil before adding sauce.

SAUCE:

**½ cup brown sugar**
**4 tablespoons cornstarch**
**2 teaspoons grated orange peel**
**1 cup orange juice**
**1 cup water**
**¼ cup lemon juice**
**1 orange, peeled, sectioned, and cut up**

Combine sugar and cornstarch. Blend in orange peel and orange juice and stir until smooth. Add water and lemon juice. Pour mixture over veal balls. Cook about 45 minutes over low heat. Gently stir in orange pieces; heat until warm, then serve.

*Makes 6 to 8 servings.*

## Osso Buco

3 tablespoons olive oil
1 minced garlic clove
4 veal shanks, 4 inches long
3 tablespoons flour
½ teaspoon paprika
½ cup dry white wine or salt-free chicken broth (see index)
1 cup water
2 tablespoons lemon juice
¼ teaspoon Tabasco sauce
¼ cup chopped parsley

Heat oil in a skillet. Add garlic and sauté. Meanwhile roll veal shanks in a mixture of flour and paprika. Add veal to skillet and brown on all sides. Pour wine or broth, water, and lemon juice over the veal. Stir in Tabasco sauce. Cover skillet and cook for about 1 hour. Add more water if necessary. Remove veal to serving platter; sprinkle with chopped parsley. Pour gravy around meat. Serve at once.

*Makes 4 servings.*

## Veal Marsala

1 pound thinly sliced veal
¼ cup flour
2 tablespoons olive oil
1 tablespoon unsalted butter or margarine
½ cup Marsala
1 tablespoon chopped parsley

Lightly dredge veal slices in flour. Heat olive oil and butter in a heavy skillet. Sauté veal slices until lightly brown. Turn and lightly brown other side. Turn heat very low. Pour the wine over the veal and sprinkle with chopped parsley. Cover and simmer for 10 minutes or until tender. Serve at once.

*Makes 4 servings.*

# Veal and Peppers

1 pound green peppers
2 tablespoons olive oil
1 sliced onion
1 crushed garlic clove
½ cup sauterne
3 tomatoes, cut in small wedges
2 pounds veal cubes
½ teaspoon oregano
⅛ teaspoon pepper
  Cooked rice (optional)

Remove stems, seeds, and membranes of the green peppers and coarsely cut up. Heat oil in a heavy skillet. Add peppers, onion, and garlic; sauté until limp. Stir in the wine. Add tomatoes, veal, oregano, and pepper. Cover and simmer for 25 minutes, stirring occasionally, until veal is tender. Serve over cooked rice, if desired.

*Makes 6 to 8 servings.*

# Broiled Lamb with Herb Marinade

6 large shoulder lamb chops
½ cup burgundy
¼ cup salad oil
½ teaspoon pepper
1½ tablespoons chopped parsley
1 garlic clove
1 small bay leaf
¼ teaspoon dried thyme
¼ teaspoon dried rosemary

Place lamb chops flat in a baking dish. Combine wine, oil, pepper, parsley, garlic, bay leaf, thyme, and rosemary;

pour over the lamb chops and cover. Refrigerate for several hours or overnight, turning chops occasionally in the marinade. Remove chops from marinade when ready to cook; place on a broiler pan, pour the marinade over the chops, and broil for 5 minutes on each side. Baste occasionally with remaining marinade.

*Makes 6 servings.*

*This recipe may be used for all sodium-restricted diets, but those restricted to 1000-, 500-, or 250-mg. low-sodium diets should omit celery from the preparations.*

## Braised Lamb Shoulder Chops

¼ cup unsalted butter or margarine
4 shoulder lamb chops, about 1-inch thick
1½ cups chopped onion
1 minced garlic clove
2 cups sliced celery
1 chopped green pepper
3 tomatoes, cut up
2 bay leaves
½ teaspoon sugar
¼ teaspoon basil
¼ teaspoon pepper

Melt butter in a large skillet. Add chops and cook until lightly browned on both sides. Add onions, garlic, celery, and green pepper. Cover and cook over low heat for 15 minutes. Add tomatoes, bay leaves, sugar, basil, and pepper. Cover and cook over low heat for 30 minutes or until lamb is tender, stirring occasionally.

*Makes 4 servings.*

# Glazed Lamb Chops

½ cup currant jelly
2 tablespoons boiling water
8 lamb rib chops
⅛ teaspoon pepper

Combine jelly and boiling water; cook over low heat, stirring constantly until jelly melts. Sprinkle lamb chops with pepper and arrange on a broiling rack. Spoon half of the jelly mixture over the chops. Broil for 5 minutes. Turn chops; coat with remaining jelly mixture. Broil 5 to 7 minutes longer or until desired degree of doneness. Serve at once.

*Makes 4 servings of 2 chops each.*

# Broiled Lamb Chops with Fruit

8 rib lamb chops
2 oranges, peeled and sectioned
4 canned pineapple rings
4 peach halves
2 tablespoons orange marmalade
2 tablespoons orange juice
2 tablespoons salad oil
2 tablespoons finely chopped onion
1 teaspoon dry mustard

Arrange lamb chops and fruit in a single layer in a baking dish. Combine marmalade, orange juice, salad oil, onion, and mustard. Pour orange mixture over all or paint the chops and fruit with a pastry brush. Cover and refrigerate for several hours. Remove chops from baking dish and place them on a broiling rack. Broil for 5 minutes, then turn and put baking dish with fruit under the broiler for an additional 5 minutes. Place the chops on a warm platter and spoon broiled fruit around chops. Serve at once.

*Makes 4 servings of 2 chops each.*

# Shish Kebab

1 finely diced onion
½ finely diced green pepper
½ teaspoon pepper
¼ teaspoon powdered sage
⅛ teaspoon dry mustard
⅛ teaspoon oregano
½ cup dry red wine
¼ cup olive oil
2 pounds lamb cubes

Combine onion, green pepper, pepper, sage, mustard, oregano, wine, and olive oil in a deep bowl. Add lamb and marinate in the refrigerator, covered, for at least 6 hours or overnight. Skewer lamb cubes and place on a broiling rack. Heat marinade in a small saucepan; brush skewered lamb with this hot marinade several times during broiling. Broil for about 5 minutes, turn, and broil an additional 5 minutes. Serve at once.

*Makes 6 servings.*

# Leg of Lamb Burgundy

**2 tablespoons dark brown sugar**
**2 tablespoons olive oil**
**1 garlic clove**
**1 leg of lamb, 6 pounds**
**¾ cup low-sodium canned tomato juice**
**1 cup burgundy**
**1 teaspoon oregano**
**⅛ teaspoon pepper**
**1 can (8¾ ounces) apricot halves**
**1 can (8¾ ounces) sliced cling peaches**

Preheat oven to 425° F. Heat brown sugar and olive oil together in a small saucepan. Cut garlic clove into slivers and insert into small slits made on the surface of the lamb. Rub meat with warm oil and sugar mixture. Place meat in a roasting pan and pour half of the tomato juice and half of the wine over it. Sprinkle with oregano and pepper. Roast in a 425° F. oven for 15 minutes. Lower the heat to 350° F. and continue roasting for a total of 18 minutes per pound (well done) or 12 minutes per pound (rare). Baste frequently with pan juices. Halfway through cooking add remaining tomato juice and wine. Place fruit in a shallow baking dish; sprinkle well with meat drippings. Bake along with roast for the last 15 minutes of cooking and serve hot with meat.

*Makes 6 servings.*

# Roasted Boned Leg of Lamb

**1 boned leg of lamb, 5 to 6 pounds**
**¼ teaspoon pepper**
**¼ cup raisins**
**¼ cup unsalted pignolia nuts**
**1 tablespoon parsley**
**1 teaspoon dillweed**
**1 tablespoon melted unsalted butter or margarine**
**1 tablespoon lemon juice**

Preheat oven to 325° F. Sprinkle the inside cavity of leg of lamb with pepper. Combine raisins, pignolia nuts, parsley, and dillweed. Place in the cavity. Drizzle with melted butter and lemon juice. Secure leg with skewers and string. Place in a shallow roasting pan and roast for 30 to 35 minutes per pound, or until meat thermometer registers 175° for medium doneness.

*Makes 8 servings.*

# Barbecued Ribs of Lamb

**3 pounds lamb riblets**
**½ cup apricot jam**
**2 tablespoons prepared mustard**
**1 teaspoon crushed rosemary**
**½ crushed garlic clove**

Preheat oven to 325° F. Place riblets on a rack in a shallow roasting pan. Bake for about 1½ hours; drain off all drippings. Combine apricot jam, mustard, rosemary, and garlic; brush mixture over ribs. Bake 30 minutes longer, turning ribs and basting with additional sauce.

*Makes 6 servings.*

# Leg of Lamb Oregano

**1 leg of lamb, 5 to 6 pounds**
**1 large clove of garlic, sliced**
**½ cup lemon juice**
**1 teaspoon oregano**
**¼ teaspoon white pepper**
**1 cup boiling water**

Preheat oven to 350° F. Make small slits in the surface of the leg of lamb; tuck a slice of garlic into each. Place roast in an uncovered roasting pan. Pour lemon juice over meat. Sprinkle with oregano and white pepper. Roast for about two hours, allowing 30 minutes per pound of meat. Remove meat from pan and set aside to rest for easier carving. To make a thin gravy, pour 1 cup boiling water into pan drippings, stirring vigorously. Cook on top of the range, stirring constantly, until gravy is reduced and of good color.

*Makes 6 to 8 servings.*

# Curried Lamb with Rice

LAMB:

**2 cups applesauce**
**2 teaspoons curry powder**
**½ teaspoon rosemary**
**2 tablespoons cornstarch**
**2 cups salt-free beef bouillon**
**6 cups cubed cooked lamb**
**4 cups cooked rice**

Combine applesauce, curry powder, rosemary, and cornstarch. Gradually add bouillon. Cook, stirring constantly, until thickened. Add lamb cubes and heat through. Mound hot rice on a platter and spoon curried lamb over the rice. Serve with apple-tomato chutney.

APPLE-TOMATO CHUTNEY:

**3 ripe tomatoes**
**1 small onion**
**½ cucumber**
**½ garlic clove**
**1 green pepper**
**1 cup applesauce**
**¾ cup cider vinegar**
**¼ cup seedless raisins**
**1¼ cups dark brown sugar**
**⅛ teaspoon crushed red pepper**
**¾ teaspoon ginger**
**¼ teaspoon cinnamon**
**¼ teaspoon nutmeg**

Wash and drain tomatoes. Scald the tomatoes and remove the skins; chop coarsely. Peel onions, cucumber, and garlic; chop. Wash the green peppers, remove the seeds, and chop. In a saucepan combine all the vegetables and the garlic with the remaining ingredients; boil until thick.

*Makes about 2½ cups of sauce.*

*This recipe may be used for all sodium-restricted diets, but those on a 1000-, 500-, or 250-mg. low-sodium diet should not eat the carrots used for flavoring.*

# Irish Stew

**3 pounds lamb cubes**
**3 cups boiling water**
**2 large sliced onions**
**1 large sliced yellow turnip**
**4 peeled carrots cut in chunks**
**4 peeled and quartered potatoes**
**4 whole peppercorns**
**½ teaspoon dried thyme**
**2 bay leaves**
**3 tablespoons flour**

Place lamb cubes and boiling water in a heavy pot; add sliced onions, cover, and simmer for 1 hour. Add turnip, carrots, potatoes, peppercorns, thyme, and bay leaves; cover and simmer 35 minutes longer. To make the gravy add enough cold water to the flour to make a thin milky paste. Add to the pot, stirring constantly until gravy thickens.

*Makes 6 to 8 servings.*

*This recipe may be used for all sodium-restricted diets, but those restricted to 1000-, 500-, or 250-mg. low-sodium diets should substitute low-sodium bread crumbs for regular bread crumbs.*

## Lamb Loaf

2 pounds ground lamb
1 grated onion
1 chopped green pepper
1 tomato
1 egg, slightly beaten
¼ cup fine dry bread crumbs
¼ teaspoon crushed rosemary
¼ teaspoon pepper

Preheat oven to 350° F. Combine ground lamb, onion, and pepper. Cut up the tomato and purée in an electric blender; add to lamb. Add beaten egg, bread crumbs, rosemary, and pepper. Mix well. Place mixture in a loaf pan and bake for 1 hour.

*Makes 6 to 8 servings.*

# Honey-Citrus Pork Chops

8 pork chops, 1-inch thick
½ cup orange juice
¼ cup lemon juice
¼ cup honey
1 teaspoon dry mustard
¼ teaspoon pepper
¼ teaspoon allspice
1 teaspoon ginger
⅛ teaspoon nutmeg

Place pork chops in a flat baking dish. Combine orange juice, lemon juice, honey, dry mustard, pepper, allspice, ginger, and nutmeg; mix well. Pour the sauce over the pork chops and marinate for several hours, turning once or twice. Place chops and sauce in the broiler, about 6 inches from heat and broil, basting frequently with sauce. Cook for 15 minutes on each side or until well done.

*Makes 8 servings.*

# Pork Chop Casserole

8 loin pork chops, ½-inch thick
  Pepper
4 tablespoons unsalted butter or margarine
1 finely diced onion
1⅓ cups enriched precooked rice
1⅓ cups water
1 cup peeled and diced tart apples
1 cup chopped prunes
¼ teaspoon pepper
¼ teaspoon poultry seasoning
¼ teaspoon sage

Preheat oven to 350° F. Trim excess fat from pork chops; sprinkle with pepper. Brown chops quickly in 2 tablespoons butter in a large skillet; drain on paper towels. Pour drippings from skillet; melt 2 tablespoons butter in skillet and sauté onion. Combine rice, water, apples, prunes, pepper, poultry seasoning, and sage in a casserole greased with unsalted butter or margarine; add sautéed onion. Mix well. Arrange pork chops on top of rice mixture. Cover and bake for 45 minutes or until chops are tender.

*Makes 4 servings.*

## Sweet and Sour Pork Chops

6 cloves
6 pork chops
1 teaspoon paprika
2 tablespoons cooking oil
1 tablespoon brown sugar
½ cup orange juice
¼ teaspoon ginger

Insert a clove in the center of each pork chop; dust surfaces of meat with paprika. Heat oil in a large skillet; brown chops on both sides over medium heat. Stir brown sugar into orange juice; add ginger. Pour over chops. Cover and simmer for 30 minutes or until fork tender.

*Makes 6 servings.*

*This recipe may be used for all sodium-restricted diets, but those restricted to 1000-, 500-, or 250-mg. low-sodium diets should substitute low-sodium bread crumbs for regular bread crumbs.*

# Fried Pork Chops and Apples

**6 well-trimmed pork chops**
**½ cup fine dry bread crumbs**
**¼ teaspoon powdered sage**
**⅛ teaspoon pepper**
**¼ cup cooking oil**
**2 apples**

Dip pork chops in a combination of the bread crumbs, sage, and pepper. Heat oil in a skillet. Brown chops on both sides and cook in hot oil for about 20 minutes or until well done. Remove chops to a warm platter. Cut apples across the core in ½-inch slices; cut out core in each slice. Fry the apple slices in the same skillet that the chops were fried in, adding a little more oil if needed. Turn apple slices when they are browned. Serve with the pork chops.

*Makes 6 servings.*

# Pork Chops with Curried Applesauce

**6 pork chops, ¾-inch thick**
**2 tablespoons unsalted butter or margarine**
**2 cups applesauce**
**½ cup apple juice**
**⅓ cup raisins**
**⅓ cup finely chopped onion**

1 teaspoon grated lemon rind
1 teaspoon curry powder
½ teaspoon ginger
¼ teaspoon nutmeg
½ cup brown sugar

Sauté pork chops in butter in a large skillet, browning both sides. Combine applesauce, apple juice, raisins, onion, lemon rind, curry powder, ginger, nutmeg, and brown sugar; pour over chops. Cover and turn heat low; cook for about 45 minutes or until chops are tender. Remove cover and cook for another 10 minutes. To serve, spoon sauce over chops.

*Makes 6 servings.*

## Boneless Pork Loin Roast

4 pounds pork loin roast, well trimmed of fat
¼ cup low-sodium peanut butter
½ cup orange juice

Preheat oven to 350° F. Place trimmed pork loin roast in a roasting pan. Roast for 2½ hours. During the last half hour of roasting, combine peanut butter and orange juice and baste pork loin with this mixture.

*Makes 6 to 8 servings.*

*This recipe may be prepared for all low-sodium diets, but those restricted to 1000-, 500-, or 250-mg. low-sodium diets should substitute low-sodium bread crumbs for regular bread crumbs.*

# Pork Patties with Mushroom-Prune Kebabs

1 pound ground pork
1 pound ground veal
¼ cup dry bread crumbs
¾ cup orange juice
1 egg
½ teaspoon grated orange peel
¼ teaspoon ground cloves
¼ cup sliced scallions
24 pitted prunes
16 mushroom caps, washed and drained
2 teaspoons cornstarch
1 teaspoon dry mustard
½ cup brown sugar
2 tablespoons vinegar

Knead together the pork and veal. Combine bread crumbs, ¼ cup orange juice, egg, orange peel, ground cloves, and sliced scallions; mix into the ground meat. Shape into 8 patties. String 3 whole prunes and 2 mushroom caps alternately on each of 8 skewers, starting and ending with prunes; set aside. Combine cornstarch, mustard, and brown sugar. Stir in ½ cup orange juice and vinegar. Heat until thickened and bubbly. Set aside for basting patties and kebabs. Broil the meat patties 13 to 18 minutes on each side over low heat, basting occasionally with sauce. Put skewers on grill for the last 5 or 6 minutes and baste with remaining sauce.

*Makes 8 servings.*

# 8

# Salt-Free Poultry

POULTRY could be regarded as the perfect protein choice for anyone with diet restrictions. It can be prepared in a number of interesting ways without sacrificing its original low-calorie, low-cholesterol, and low-sodium qualities. Add to that its comparatively low cost and you'll find this to be a favorite chapter of recipes.

Sodium-restricted dieters should not be served canned or frozen prepared chicken dinners, turkey dinners, or smoked turkey. In addition, it would be wise to cut away all skin and fat before serving poultry to the low-cholesterol dieter.

When preparing duckling, be sure to roast fifteen minutes at very high heat to quickly melt the fat layer under the skin. Then reduce the heat and roast until the duckling is crisp, pricking the skin from time to time to release the fat. It is helpful to prop up the bird on a roasting rack set in a large pan allowing the fat to run off. The low-cholesterol dieter should cut away the skin and any remaining fat.

Read frozen turkey roll labels carefully to see whether any sodium has been added in the processing. Check the labels of frozen whole birds, too, as many are now self-basting and may have sodium in the added ingredients.

All poultry has about 25 milligrams of sodium to three ounces of cooked meat. You can roughly figure that a three-ounce portion is equal to one serving of a leg or thigh of chicken, or one-half of a chicken breast. Whether you stew it, fry it, or broil it, chicken can be served in many delicious ways several times a week.

# Roasted Orange Chicken

**2 broiler chickens, about 3 pounds each**
**1 cup orange juice**
**¼ teaspoon white pepper**
  **Paprika**

Preheat oven to 350° F. Wash, dry, and arrange chickens in a roasting pan. Pour orange juice over the chicken, covering all sides. Sprinkle with pepper and paprika. Roast uncovered for 1¼ hours, basting with pan juices or additional orange juice after about 35 minutes of roasting time. Cut chickens in quarters to serve.

*Makes 8 servings.*

*This recipe may be used for all sodium-restricted diets, but those restricted to 500- or 250-mg. low-sodium diets should substitute low-sodium bread crumbs for regular bread crumbs.*

# Baked Chicken with Herbs

**2 broiler chickens, quartered**
**¼ teaspoon pepper**
**½ cup unsalted butter or margarine, softened**
**1 crushed garlic clove**
**1 cup fine dry bread crumbs**
**¼ cup chopped parsley**
**1 teaspoon rosemary**
**½ teaspoon dry mustard**

Preheat oven to 375° F. Sprinkle chicken parts lightly with pepper. Combine butter and garlic. On a piece of waxed paper, combine bread crumbs, parsley, rosemary, and dry mustard. Spread chicken quarters on both sides with butter and garlic mixture; dip in bread crumb mixture and coat well. Place on foil-lined baking pan. Bake for 1 hour or until chicken is tender.

*Makes 8 servings.*

*This recipe may be used for all low sodium-restricted diets, but those restricted to 1000-, 500-, or 250-mg. low-sodium diets should not eat the celery and carrots used for flavoring.*

## Stewed Chicken

1 broiler chicken, cut up
3 cups water
2 tablespoons lemon juice
1 teaspoon sugar
⅛ teaspoon pepper
1 bay leaf
½ cup sliced celery
1 package (10 ounces) salt-free frozen peas
6 carrots, pared and quartered
12 small white onions
5 tablespoons flour
3 tablespoons water

Place chicken parts in a heavy saucepan. Add water, lemon juice, sugar, pepper, bay leaf, and celery. Cover; bring to a boil. Reduce heat and simmer for 30 minutes. Add peas, carrots, and onions. Simmer 30 minutes more. Blend together the flour and water making a smooth paste; blend in a small amount of the hot broth, then return the mixture to the broth in the saucepan. Stirring constantly, bring to a boil and cook for several minutes.

*Makes 4 servings.*

*This recipe may be used for all sodium-restricted diets, but those restricted to 1000-, 500-, or 250-mg. low-sodium diets should not eat the carrots and celery used to flavor this recipe.*

## Oven-Baked Chicken Stew

2 broiler chickens, about 3 pounds each
½ teaspoon garlic, powdered
¼ teaspoon white pepper
2 large fresh dillweed sprigs
1 cup dry sauterne
2 tomatoes, peeled and cut up
4 carrots, scraped and cut into 1-inch chunks
4 potatoes, pared and quartered
4 celery stalks, cut into 1-inch chunks
1 package (10 ounces) frozen cut green beans
1 large onion, sliced

Preheat oven to 350° F. Wash, dry, and place whole chickens in a Dutch oven. Sprinkle with garlic and pepper and add the dill. Pour the wine in the bottom of the Dutch oven. Place the vegetables around the chickens. Cover tightly and bake for 1½ hours or until chicken is fork tender. To serve, cut chicken in quarters and spoon the vegetables on top.

*Makes 8 servings.*

## Sherried Chicken Thighs

8 chicken thighs
¼ teaspoon paprika
¾ cup salt-free chicken broth (see index)
¼ cup sherry

1 sliced onion
½ thinly sliced green pepper
¼ teaspoon dried dillweed
  Cooked rice or cooked noodles (optional)

Sprinkle chicken thighs with paprika and broil on both sides for 10 minutes. In a skillet combine chicken broth, sherry, onion, green pepper, and dillweed; simmer for 5 minutes. Add broiled chicken thighs. Cover and cook 10 minutes. Serve on rice or noodles, if desired.

*Makes 4 servings.*

## Chicken Turmeric

1 broiler chicken, cut into serving portions
⅓ cup flour
1 teaspoon turmeric
½ teaspoon black pepper
⅛ teaspoon mace
½ cup unsalted butter or margarine
½ cup hot water
1 teaspoon tarragon
¼ cup dry white wine

Wash the chicken and wipe dry. Combine flour, turmeric, pepper, and mace; dredge the chicken, coating well. Brown on all sides in a heavy skillet in hot butter. Push chicken to one side and stir any remaining seasoned flour into the pan butter. Add hot water and mix well. Evenly distribute the chicken in the skillet and sprinkle with tarragon; then drizzle with wine. Cover; reduce heat to a simmer and cook for 45 minutes or until tender. Add extra water if needed. Serve hot.

*Makes 4 servings.*

*This recipe may be used for all sodium-restricted diets, but those restricted to 500- or 250-mg. low-sodium diets should substitute low-sodium milk for regular milk.*

# Chicken Paprikash

2 broiler chickens, cut into serving portions
½ teaspoon pepper
½ cup flour
¼ cup unsalted butter, margarine, or shortening
2⅓ tablespoons paprika
1 finely diced onion
2 cups boiling water
3 tablespoons cornstarch
1 cup milk

Dredge the chicken pieces in a combination of pepper and flour. Brown in melted shortening in a heavy skillet. Sprinkle 2 tablespoons paprika evenly over chicken. Add onion and boiling water; cover and simmer for 1½ hours, or until chicken is tender. Remove chicken to serving platter. Stir the cornstarch into the milk; add the remaining 1 teaspoon paprika. Stir into liquid in pan and cook until thickened, stirring constantly. Pour over chicken.

*Makes 8 servings.*

## Sesame Chicken Breasts and Mushrooms

**4 whole chicken breasts**
**3 tablespoons unsalted butter or margarine**
**¼ cup flour**
**½ teaspoon paprika**
**2 tablespoons sesame seeds**
**½ pound sliced fresh mushrooms**
**½ cup dry sherry**

Remove the bones from the chicken breasts; split in half and then split each half into two thin cutlets. Melt butter in a large skillet. Combine flour, paprika, and sesame seeds; lightly dust the chicken pieces and fry in the melted butter. Brown on both sides. Cover the chicken with the sliced mushrooms. Pour sherry over the chicken and mushrooms, cover the skillet, and cook over very low heat for 20 minutes.

*Makes 6 to 8 servings.*

## Lemonade Broiled Chicken

**1 broiler chicken, quartered**
**2 cups lemonade, frozen and reconstituted**
**¼ teaspoon rosemary**
**¼ teaspoon paprika**

Marinate chicken parts in lemonade for one hour. Remove the chicken and place in a broiling pan skin side down. Sprinkle with rosemary and paprika. Broil for 10 minutes. Turn over and sprinkle with additional paprika, if desired. Broil for 10 minutes more or until cooked through.

*Makes 4 servings.*

# Broiled Mandarin Chicken

1 broiler chicken, quartered
1 tablespoon unsalted butter or margarine
¼ teaspoon paprika
1 tablespoon cornstarch
⅛ teaspoon rosemary
⅛ teaspoon marjoram
1 small can mandarin oranges

Dot chicken with butter, sprinkle with paprika, and arrange in a broiling pan. Broil skin side down for 10 minutes, then turn and broil another 10 minutes or until cooked through. Meanwhile, combine cornstarch, rosemary, and marjoram in a small saucepan; add liquid from mandarin oranges and stir until smooth. Cook until there is a thick sauce; add orange slices. Pour over broiled chicken just before serving.

*Makes 4 servings.*

*This recipe may be prepared for all low-sodium diets; but those restricted to 1000-, 500-, or 250-mg. low-sodium diets should substitute low-sodium milk for the evaporated milk and increase the flour to 4 tablespoons. If serving on toast points, those on 500- or 250-mg. low-sodium diets should substitute low-sodium bread for regular bread.*

## Creamed Chicken

3 tablespoons unsalted butter or margarine
¼ pound sliced mushrooms
1 tablespoon chopped onion
¼ cup chopped green pepper
3 tablespoons flour
⅛ teaspoon ground allspice
⅛ teaspoon pepper
½ cup salt-free chicken broth (see index)
1⅔ cups evaporated milk
2 cups diced cooked chicken
  Toast points (optional)

In a medium-sized saucepan melt butter over low heat. Add mushrooms, onion, and green pepper; cook until green pepper is tender (about 3 minutes). Remove from heat. Sprinkle in flour a little at a time, blending until smooth. Add allspice and pepper. Stir in chicken broth and evaporated milk. Cook and stir over medium heat until thickened. Add chicken and heat through. Serve on toast points, if desired.

*Makes 6 servings.*

# Chicken Fruit Skillet

2 tablespoons unsalted butter or margarine
2 whole chicken breasts, boned, skinned,
    and cut into 1½-inch chunks
¼ cup chopped onion
¼ teaspoon dried tarragon
⅛ teaspoon pepper
¼ cup orange juice
½ cup halved and seeded dark grapes
2 bananas

Melt butter in a large skillet. Add chicken chunks and cook over moderately high heat until white, stirring frequently. Add onion and cook 1 minute. Add tarragon and pepper. Stir in orange juice. Cover and cook 15 minutes. Stir in grapes. Peel and slice bananas, add to the chicken, and heat.

*Makes 4 servings.*

*This recipe may be prepared for all low-sodium diets. If serving on toast points those restricted to 500- or 250-mg. low-sodium diets should substitute low-sodium bread for regular bread.*

# Chicken Livers and Mushrooms

1 pound fresh chicken livers
1 sliced onion
1 pound sliced mushrooms
2 tablespoons unsalted butter or margarine

⅛ teaspoon pepper
¼ cup sherry
 Toast points or cooked rice (optional)

Sauté chicken livers, sliced onion, and sliced mushrooms in butter, stirring frequently, until the chicken livers are tender. Sprinkle with pepper and pour the sherry over all. Serve on toast points or cooked rice, if desired.

*Makes 4 servings.*

# Fruit-Glazed Turkey Roll

1 frozen turkey roll, 4 pounds
½ cup undiluted frozen pineapple-orange
   juice concentrate
⅓ cup sugar
½ teaspoon thyme
1 cup water
1 tablespoon cornstarch

Roast turkey roll according to package directions. Thaw out the juice concentrate and combine with sugar and thyme in a small saucepan; heat to dissolve the sugar. During the last half hour of roasting, baste the turkey roll with the sugar and juice mixture. Remove turkey roll when done. Add the remaining sugar and juice mixture to drippings in pan. Add water mixed with cornstarch and bring to a boil, stirring constantly. Serve over the turkey roll.

*Makes 6 to 8 servings.*

# Turkey with Apricot Brandy Glaze

1 large turkey, 12 or more pounds
1 garlic clove
¼ pound unsalted butter or margarine
½ cup apricot brandy
  Boiling water
½ cup cold water
2 tablespoons cornstarch

Preheat oven to 325° F. Clean, wash, and dry the turkey. Place in a large open roasting pan. Peel and cut garlic clove in half; rub the cut edges over the inside and outside of the turkey; discard garlic. Melt butter in a small saucepan; add apricot brandy. With a pastry brush paint the skin of the turkey with some of this mixture. Place a loose tent of aluminum foil over the top of the turkey and place in the preheated oven. Paint with the remainder of the apricot brandy glaze once an hour throughout the cooking time (allow 15 to 20 minutes per pound). When turkey leg jiggles easily, it is done. To make pan gravy, remove turkey to a platter and cover to keep warm; pour boiling water into roasting pan, stirring all the residue. Add any remaining apricot glaze. Heat and stir until all the residue has been worked into the boiling water. (To thicken, stir ½ cup cold water into 2 tablespoons cornstarch, then stir this mixture into the gravy and cook for 2 or 3 minutes, until gravy is thickened.) Slice turkey and serve with gravy.

*A 12-pound turkey will serve 8 people.*

# Turkey with Chive Rice

**4 cups diced, cooked turkey**
**½ cup honey**
**½ teaspoon dry mustard**
**1 teaspoon curry powder**
**4 tablespoons turkey drippings**
**2 cups cooked white rice**
**2 tablespoons chopped chives**

The turkey may be cooked on top of the range or baked in the oven. Spread diced, cooked turkey in a large skillet or a shallow baking pan. Mix together the honey, mustard, curry powder, and turkey drippings. Mix with the diced turkey. Sauté turkey mixture, stirring occasionally, or bake at 350° F. until hot (about 30 minutes) stirring once or twice. Place cooked rice in a heated serving dish and spoon the turkey mixture over the rice. Sprinkle with chopped chives.

*Makes 4 servings.*

# Cornish Hens with Lemon-Apple Glaze

CORNISH HENS:

**4 Cornish hens, 1 pound each**
 **Giblets from hens**
**2 cups cooked rice**
**1 tablespoon chopped parsley**
**¼ cup white seedless raisins**
 **Unsalted butter or margarine (optional)**

Preheat oven to 375° F. Arrange washed and cleaned hens in a small roasting pan. Place giblets in a small saucepan; cover with water and simmer until tender. Remove from pan with slotted spoon. Chop the giblets and add them to cooked rice. Add parsley and raisins. Stuff the mixture into the cavities of the hens. Fold wing tips back under the breasts of the hens and secure the legs with cord. Rub skin with butter, if desired, and bake in the preheated oven for 1 hour, basting occasionally with juices in pan. While the Cornish hens are baking, prepare the glaze.

*Makes 4 servings.*

GLAZE:

**1 tablespoon cornstarch**
**2 tablespoons sugar**
**1 cup apple juice**
**½ teaspoon cinnamon**
**3 lemon slices**

Combine cornstarch and sugar in a small saucepan. Add ¼ cup apple juice to make a smooth paste. Add remaining apple juice and cook and stir over medium heat until slightly thickened. Add cinnamon and lemon slices. During the last half hour of baking brush the hens with the lemon-apple glaze several times. Serve extra sauce over hens.

# 9

# Salt-Free Fish

F RESH fish is the only kind of fish allowed on a low sodium-restricted diet, except for canned low-sodium dietetic fish and salmon. No regular canned tuna or salmon, canned anchovies, sardines, tomato herring, clams, shrimp, oysters, crabmeat, or caviar are allowed.

Fresh fish is an important ingredient in a healthier diet for the whole family, but especially for the patient who is concerned with low-sodium, low cholesterol, and low calorie cooking. The bonus is that fish cooks quickly and is easily digestible, too.

Lemon has a natural affinity for fish, so be sure to have a good supply of fresh lemons at all times. Parsley, dill, and other herbs all also pep up the taste. Fish is a versatile and delicious source of protein when you learn to cook it with care.

Since fish has to be cooked the same day you buy it, for best flavor results, plan your menus and marketing strategy in advance. Be sure that the fish you buy is fresh—if whole, look at the eyes to see if they are bright, clear, and bulging. Press the skin to be sure the pressure leaves no mark of indentation. See that the gills are bright red. Sniff to be sure that there is only the fresh odor of the sea. When you get home, refrigerate fish immediately until it is ready to be cooked.

Here follows a whole collection of delicious fish recipes to pamper your patient's palate.

*This recipe may be prepared for all low-sodium diets, but those restricted to 1000-, 500-, or 250-mg. low-sodium diets should omit the sour cream.*

# Banana-Topped Sole

**4 large fillets of sole**
**1 large banana**
**2 tablespoons lemon juice**
**¼ cup dairy sour cream**
**¼ teaspoon paprika**

Grease a baking dish with unsalted butter or margarine and arrange fillets flat on it. Slice the bananas and toss with lemon juice; dot top of fish with banana slices. Spread a thin layer of sour cream over the banana slices. Sprinkle with paprika. Broil for about 10 minutes or until the fish flakes easily. Serve at once.

*Makes 4 servings.*

## Flounder Florentine

**4 thin slices fillet of flounder**
**1 package (10 ounces) frozen chopped spinach, thawed**
**1 tablespoon grated onion**
**¼ teaspoon nutmeg**
**1 tablespoon unsalted butter or margarine**
**¼ cup lemon juice**
**1 tablespoon chopped dill**

Preheat oven to 350° F. Cut each slice of fish in half lengthwise. Combine thawed chopped spinach, onion, and nutmeg. Spread the mixture on the fish slices, roll each up like a jelly roll, and fasten with toothpicks. Place in a baking dish that has been greased with unsalted butter or margarine. Heat butter in a small saucepan; add lemon juice and chopped dill. Spoon butter mixture over fish. Bake uncovered for about 25 minutes or until fish flakes easily.

*Makes 4 servings.*

*This recipe may be used for mild sodium-restricted diets only. Those restricted to 1000-, 500-, or 250-mg. low-sodium diets should omit the shrimp in the sauce.*

# Baked Sea Bass with Shrimp Sauce

SEA BASS:

3 tablespoons salad oil
1 tablespoon wine vinegar
1 cleaned sea bass, 4 pounds
2 tablespoons unsalted butter or margarine
¼ cup water

Preheat oven to 350° F. Combine the oil and vinegar. Wipe the inside and outside of the cleaned fish with the oil and vinegar mixture. Pour a little water around the fish and cover the pan tightly with foil or with a tightly fitted lid. In a small saucepan melt 2 tablespoons butter and stir in ¼ cup water. Use this mixture to baste the fish occasionally. Bake for 1 hour in the preheated oven. When fish flakes easily, remove pan from oven and place fish on a warm platter.

SHRIMP SAUCE:

Boiling water
2 tablespoons unsalted butter or margarine
1 tablespoon flour
Juice of half a lemon
½ teaspoon paprika
¼ cup cooked shrimp, finely chopped

Pour a small amount of boiling water into the pan in which the fish was baked to loosen the residue, then strain this into a saucepan. Melt 2 tablespoons butter in a skillet and add the flour, stirring constantly as it cooks for a few moments. Then spoon a little of the fish gravy into the butter and flour mixture, stirring until smooth. Pour this mixture back into the gravy and simmer, stirring constantly. Add lemon juice, paprika, and chopped shrimp. Pour into a gravy boat to serve with the fish.

*Makes 4 servings.*

*This recipe may be used for mild sodium-restricted diets only. Those restricted to 1000-, 500-, or 250-mg. low-sodium diets should omit this recipe.*

## Shrimp in Green Sauce

3 tablespoons unsalted butter or margarine
¼ cup finely chopped parsley
¼ cup finely chopped watercress
1 small minced garlic clove
½ cup finely chopped onion
1 pound shelled and deveined raw shrimp
⅛ teaspoon Tabasco sauce
3 tablespoons lemon juice

Melt butter in a skillet; add parsley, watercress, garlic, and onion and cook until onion is tender. Add shrimp, Tabasco sauce, and lemon juice. Cover; continue cooking 3 to 5 minutes, or until shrimp are pink and cooked through.

*Makes 4 servings (main course).*
*Makes 8 servings (appetizer).*

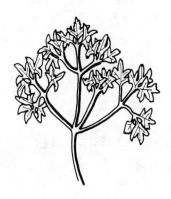

*This recipe may be used for all sodium-restricted diets, but those restricted to 500- or 250-mg. low-sodium diets should substitute low-sodium milk for regular milk.*

## Fried Trout

**4 small trout, about ½ pound each**
**1 cup milk**
**½ cup flour**
**½ teaspoon paprika**
**3 tablespoons olive oil**
**3 tablespoons unsalted butter or margarine**
**4 tablespoons chopped parsley**
**4 thin lemon slices**

Wash and dry the cleaned whole trout. Place in a small flat dish, add the milk, and soak for a half hour. Remove the trout from the milk and dredge in a mixture of flour and paprika. Heat olive oil and butter in a large skillet. Fry the trout for about 5 minutes on each side. Remove to a warm platter. Sprinkle each with about 1 tablespoon of chopped parsley and top with a slice of lemon.

*Makes 4 servings.*

## Baked Cod Fillets

**2 pounds cod fillets**
**2 tablespoons salad oil**
**½ teaspoon paprika**
**2 tablespoons unsalted butter or margarine**

1 small diced onion
1 small minced garlic clove
3 tomatoes, cut up
½ cup dry white wine
1 teaspoon sugar
⅛ teaspoon pepper

Preheat oven to 350° F. Paint the cod fillets with salad oil on all sides; arrange in one layer in a baking dish. Sprinkle with paprika. Melt butter in a small saucepan; sauté onion and garlic for several minutes. Add tomatoes, white wine, sugar, and pepper. Stir and simmer for several minutes. Pour this mixture over the fish. Bake for about 30 minutes or until fish flakes easily.

*Makes 4 servings.*

## Sweet-and-Sour Whitefish

2 large sliced onions
2 cups water
½ cup tarragon vinegar
½ cup sugar
1 teaspoon ground ginger
½ teaspoon pepper
3 pounds whitefish steaks

Place onions and water in a heavy saucepan; simmer for 10 minutes. Add vinegar, sugar, ginger, and pepper; simmer for 5 minutes more. Turn off heat. Place fish steaks in the mixture and let this marinate for about 10 minutes, adding more water if necessary to cover fish. Bring mixture to a boil, cover, reduce heat, and simmer for 35 to 45 minutes or until fish flakes easily. Add additional water if necessary to keep fish covered.

*Makes 4 servings.*

*This recipe may be used for all sodium-restricted diets, but those restricted to 500- or 250-mg. low-sodium diets should substitute low-sodium bread for regular bread and low-sodium milk for regular milk.*

# Stuffed Baked Bluefish

1 whole bluefish, about 4 pounds, cleaned
2 tablespoons unsalted butter or margarine
1 small onion, diced
1 cup dry bread, torn up
1 apple, peeled and diced
½ cup white raisins
2 tablespoons chopped parsley
¼ cup milk
1 egg, beaten
¼ teaspoon thyme
⅛ teaspoon pepper
   Juice of one lemon

Preheat oven to 375° F. Wash and wipe bluefish dry. In a saucepan, melt butter and sauté diced onion until golden and translucent. Add the bread, diced apple, raisins, and parsley. Combine milk and egg; add to the bread mixture. Add thyme and pepper. Stir lightly so mixture does not pack down; fill cavity of fish with this mixture. Place fish in a baking dish that has been greased with unsalted butter or margarine. Squeeze lemon juice over the fish. Bake for about 45 minutes or until fish flakes easily.

*Makes 4 servings.*

*This recipe may be used for all sodium-restricted diets, but those restricted to 1000-, 500-, or 250-mg. low-sodium diets should omit the sour cream, spreading fish with additional unsalted butter or margarine instead.*

## Fillet of Sole Rolls

4 medium fillets of sole
½ cup dairy sour cream
2 tablespoons chopped chives
2 sliced tomatoes
½ cup white wine
½ teaspoon paprika
⅛ teaspoon pepper
2 tablespoons unsalted butter or margarine

Preheat oven to 350° F. Spread one side of each fillet with a mixture of sour cream and chopped chives; roll up. Grease a baking dish with unsalted butter or margarine and arrange rolls in it. Place sliced tomatoes around rolls. Pour wine over fish. Sprinkle with paprika and pepper. Dot with butter. Cover dish and bake for 20 minutes or until fillets flake easily.

*Makes 4 servings.*

# Broiled Salmon Steaks

**4 salmon steaks, about 1-inch thick**
**½ cup salad oil**
**¼ teaspoon tarragon**
**⅛ teaspoon pepper**
**2 tablespoons melted unsalted butter or margarine**
  **Lemon slices**
  **Parsley**

Wipe steaks dry and lay them in a mixture of salad oil, tarragon, and pepper for at least one hour. Then drain and place them on a broiling pan. Broil for at least 20 minutes, basting frequently with the melted butter. Serve with lemon slices and parsley.

*Makes 4 servings.*

# Boiled Salmon Steaks

**4 salmon steaks**
  **Boiling water**
**2 tablespoons wine vinegar**
**4 whole peppercorns**
**1 bay leaf**
  **Lemon slices**
  **Parsley sprigs**

Arrange salmon steaks in a large skillet. Pour boiling water over to cover fish. Add vinegar, peppercorns, and bay leaf. Bring to a boil and cook, allowing about 12 minutes per pound of fish. When fish flakes easily, remove it with a slotted spatula. Garnish with lemon slices and parsley sprigs.

*Makes 4 servings.*

# Baked Haddock

1 pound haddock fillets
½ onion, diced
1 minced garlic clove
1 tablespoon unsalted butter or margarine
1 can (8 ounces) low-sodium tomatoes
½ teaspoon sugar
1 tablespoon lemon juice
¼ teaspoon crushed dried basil

Preheat oven to 400° F. Arrange fish in a baking pan that has been greased with unsalted butter or margarine. In a small skillet, sauté onion and garlic in butter. Meanwhile, pour tomatoes into an electric blender and blend smooth; add sugar, lemon juice, and basil. Blend again. Pour mixture into skillet with onions; stir and cook for 2 minutes. Pour over fish. Bake for 20 minutes or until fish flakes easily.

*Makes 2 to 3 servings.*

*This recipe may be used for all sodium-restricted diets, but those restricted to 500- or 250-mg. low-sodium diets should substitute low-sodium milk for regular milk.*

# Baked Halibut

4 halibut steaks
1 tablespoon unsalted butter or margarine, softened
⅛ teaspoon white pepper
1 cup milk
1 sprig dillweed, finely chopped

Preheat oven to 350° F. Rub halibut steaks with butter. Sprinkle with pepper. Arrange in a baking dish. Pour milk around the fish and sprinkle with dillweed. Bake for 30 minutes or until fish flakes easily. Baste with the milk every ten minutes while cooking.

*Makes 4 servings.*

# Steamed Red Snapper

**2 thinly sliced tomatoes**
**1 large diced onion**
**2 tablespoons unsalted butter or margarine**
**1 lemon, cut in thin slices**
**1 cleaned red snapper, 4 pounds**
  **Parsley**

Arrange tomatoes and onion in the top half of a steaming unit (see Note below). Place dots of butter and some of the lemon slices in the cavity of the washed and dried fish. Add the fish to the steaming unit and place unit over boiling water. Steam about one hour. Open the steamer once and carefully turn the fish over. Serve with remaining lemon slices and parsley sprigs. Spoon cooked tomatoes and onion around the fish.

NOTE: If no steaming unit is available, bake the fish in a baking dish in a 350° F. oven for 45 minutes. Omit turning the fish.

*Makes 4 servings.*

# Lemon-Broiled Fillet of Sole

**4 slices fillet of sole**
**½ cup lemon juice**
**2 tablespoons grated onion**
**2 teaspoons chopped fresh parsley**
  **Paprika**

Arrange fish slices in a single layer in a large flat baking pan. Pour lemon juice over the fish. Sprinkle with onion, parsley, and paprika. (The fish may be prepared up to two hours before broiling; however, refrigerate, covered, until ready to broil.) Broil for about 7 minutes, or until fish is lightly browned and flakes easily. Serve at once.

*Makes 4 servings.*

*This recipe may be used for mild sodium-restricted diets only. Those restricted to 1000-, 500-, or 250-mg. low-sodium diets should omit this recipe.*

# Scampi

**1 pound shrimp, peeled and deveined with tails intact**
**¼ cup olive oil**
**1 crushed garlic clove**
**1 tablespoon chopped parsley**

Roll shrimp in a mixture of olive oil, crushed garlic, and chopped parsley. Arrange on a broiler pan. Slip under the broiler for 5 minutes or until shrimp are pink.

*Makes 4 servings.*

*This recipe may be used for mild sodium-restricted diets only. Those restricted to 1000-, 500-, or 250-mg. low-sodium diets should omit this recipe.*

# Shrimp Creole

2 tablespoons olive oil
2 sliced onions
1 crushed garlic clove
1 tablespoon flour
1 teaspoon sugar
1 tablespoon chili powder
1 cup water
2 tomatoes, cut into small wedges
1 package (10 ounces) salt-free frozen peas
2 cups cooked shrimp
1 tablespoon vinegar

Heat oil in a heavy saucepan. Sauté onions and garlic in oil for several minutes. Form a paste of the flour, sugar, and chili powder with some of the water; stir it into the onion mixture. Slowly add the remaining water, stirring constantly. Simmer uncovered for 15 minutes. Add tomatoes and peas. Simmer until they are cooked through. Add shrimp and vinegar; stir until heated through.

*Makes 4 servings.*

# 10

# Salt-Free Vegetables

V EGETABLE dishes are a rainbow of color to brighten your platters and these recipes include some herb ideas to fascinate the fussiest of eaters. Most ½-cup servings of vegetables have about 9 milligrams of sodium, making it possible to serve several varieties at each meal.

Omit all canned vegetables or vegetable juices, except those with labels marked "low-sodium dietetic". You may use all frozen vegetables, except those which have had sauces added, or those processed with salt. Watch out particularly for frozen peas and lima beans—check the labels to be sure that they have not been processed with salt.

Because of high natural content of sodium, avoid the use of artichokes, beets and their greens, carrots, celery, Swiss chard, dandelion greens, hominy, kale, mustard greens, sauerkraut, spinach, and white turnips. While those on a mild sodium-restricted diet may eat some of these vegetables, those on a low-sodium-restricted diet of 1000-, 500-, or 250-mg. should not eat any of these vegetables, although they may be used for flavoring cooked soups, meat, and poultry dishes.

There is no need for vegetables to be dreary—a pinch of this and that will provide a zesty flavor. The recipes in this chapter were constructed to give the sodium-diet patient pure pleasure.

# Asparagus with Lemon-Butter Sauce

**1 pound fresh asparagus, trimmed**
**¼ cup lemon juice**
**2 tablespoons unsalted butter or margarine, melted**
**1 tablespoon chopped parsley**

Plunge fresh asparagus into boiling water for 1 minute. Then plunge asparagus into a waiting bowl of ice water until ready to cook. (This method preserves the bright green color for several hours.) Cook asparagus covered with water, or place it in a steaming unit, for 10 to 15 minutes or until fork tender. Drain. Combine lemon juice, butter, and chopped parsley; pour over the asparagus and serve.

*Makes 4 to 6 servings.*

# Baked Acorn Squash

**2 acorn squash**
**2 teaspoons unsalted butter or margarine**
**2 teaspoons brown sugar**
**¼ teaspoon cinnamon**

Preheat oven to 350° F. Cut acorn squash in half lengthwise. Scoop out and discard seeds. Place squash, cut side up, in a baking pan. Fill cavities with dots of butter, brown sugar, and cinnamon. Bake for 25 to 30 minutes or until fork tender.

*Makes 4 servings.*

## Acorn Squash Rings with Peas

**1 acorn squash**
**1 teaspoon sugar**
**1 package (10 ounces) salt-free frozen peas**
**1 tablespoon unsalted butter or margarine**
**⅛ teaspoon rosemary**

Slice acorn squash crosswise into 1-inch rings. Remove and discard seeds. Cook rings in a covered skillet with a small amount of water until tender. Drain and sprinkle with sugar. Meanwhile, cook peas as directed on the package; drain and toss with butter and rosemary. Arrange squash rings on a platter and fill the cavities with peas.

*Makes 6 servings.*

## Green Beans Oregano

**1 pound fresh green beans, trimmed and sliced**
**3 tomatoes, cut in small wedges**
**1 small onion, sliced**
**½ teaspoon sugar**
**⅛ teaspoon white pepper**
**¼ teaspoon oregano**

Place green beans in a heavy saucepan. Add 1 inch of water. Add tomato wedges, onion, sugar, pepper, and oregano. Cook until beans are tender (about 15 minutes). Drain and serve.

*Makes 6 servings.*

# Green Beans and Tomatoes

1 pound fresh green beans, trimmed and sliced
2 tomatoes, cut in wedges
1 small onion, diced
½ teaspoon sugar
¼ teaspoon thyme
⅛ teaspoon pepper
1 cup water
2 tablespoons unsalted butter or margarine

Place green beans in a heavy saucepan. Add tomatoes, onion, sugar, thyme, pepper, and water. Cook until beans are tender (about 15 minutes). Drain. Add butter and toss lightly.

*Makes 6 servings.*

# Wax Beans Amandine

1 pound wax beans
3 tablespoons unsalted butter or margarine
¼ cup sliced blanched unsalted almonds
½ teaspoon marjoram
⅛ teaspoon pepper

Trim ends of wax beans and place in a large saucepan; cover with water and cook over low heat until tender. Drain. Meanwhile, in a small saucepan, melt butter. Add almonds and heat over medium heat, stirring occasionally until almonds are light brown. Add marjoram and pepper. Cook a minute more and pour over drained cooked beans. Serve at once.

*Makes 6 to 8 servings.*

# Herbed Peas

**1 pound fresh shelled peas**
**2 chopped parsley sprigs**
**¼ teaspoon chervil**
**¼ teaspoon thyme**
**1 tablespoon unsalted butter or margarine**

Place peas in a saucepan and cover with cold water. Add parsley, chervil, and thyme. Cook over low heat for about 10 minutes or until tender. Drain. Toss lightly with butter.

*Makes 4 to 6 servings.*

*This recipe may be used for mild sodium-restricted diets only. Those restricted to 1000-, 500-, or 250-mg. low-sodium diets must omit this recipe.*

# Beets L'Orange

**1 can (8 ounces) low-sodium beets**
**1 teaspoon grated orange peel**
**1 tablespoon grated onion**
**¼ teaspoon dried dillweed**

Empty beets and the juice from the can into a saucepan. Add grated orange rind, onion, and dillweed. Simmer, covered, for 5 minutes.

*Makes 2 servings.*

# Broccoli with Parsley-Butter Sauce

**2 packages (10 ounces each) frozen broccoli,**
  **or 2 heavy stalks fresh broccoli**
**2 tablespoons unsalted butter or margarine**
**1 tablespoon lemon juice**
**1 tablespoon chopped parsley**

Cook broccoli according to package directions, and then drain. (If using fresh broccoli, trim well and pare stalk of its thin tough outer covering so it will cook faster; slice lengthwise into thin strips. Cover with water and cook until tender; about 15 minutes. Drain.) Melt butter and stir in lemon juice and parsley. Pour over drained broccoli. Serve at once.

*Makes 6 servings.*

# Brussels Sprouts

**1 package (10 ounces) frozen brussels sprouts**
**1 cup water**
**1 teaspoon chopped parsley**
**½ teaspoon sugar**
**¼ teaspoon dried marjoram**
**⅛ teaspoon white pepper**
**1 tablespoon unsalted butter or margarine**

Cut brussels sprouts in half lengthwise and place in a saucepan with the water, parsley, sugar, marjoram, and pepper. Cook for 5 minutes or until tender but not mushy. Drain. Toss lightly with butter and serve.

*Makes 4 servings.*

*This recipe may be used for mild sodium-restricted diets only. Those restricted to 1000-, 500-, or 250-mg. low-sodium diets must omit this recipe.*

## Glazed Carrots

**1 pound fresh slender carrots**
**¼ cup orange juice**
**2 tablespoons unsalted butter or margarine**
**2 tablespoons brown sugar**

Cut carrots into oval disks by slanting the knife as you cut. Cover with water in a covered saucepan and cook until fork tender. Drain. Pour orange juice over carrots and toss. Add butter and brown sugar. Simmer and stir until butter and sugar are melted and carrots appear glazed (about 3 minutes).

*Makes 4 to 6 servings.*

## Sweet 'n' Sour Red Cabbage

**1 medium-sized red cabbage, shredded**
**1 onion, sliced**
**1 apple, pared and sliced**
**⅓ cup brown sugar**
**2 tablespoons red wine vinegar**
**½ cup water**
**1 tablespoon lemon juice**
**¼ teaspoon ground ginger**

Place cabbage, onion, and apple in a heavy saucepan. Add brown sugar, vinegar, water, lemon juice, and ginger. Cover and simmer for 1½ to 2 hours, adding more water if needed.

*Makes 6 servings.*

# Cauliflower

1 head cauliflower
2 tablespoons lemon juice
¼ teaspoon marjoram
¼ teaspoon paprika

Wash and trim cauliflower. Place in a heavy saucepan with about an inch of water. Add lemon juice and marjoram. Cover and simmer until tender. Drain. Place cauliflower on a platter. Sprinkle with paprika. Serve at once.

*Makes 6 to 8 servings.*

# Broiled Stuffed Mushrooms

8 large mushrooms
¼ cup ground beef
1 tablespoon chopped parsley
⅛ teaspoon white pepper
⅛ teaspoon ground cinnamon

Preheat oven to 350° F. Remove stems from mushrooms; wash caps and set aside. Chop stems. Combine chopped mushroom stems, ground beef, parsley, pepper, and cinnamon. Stuff mixture into mushroom caps. Place mushrooms, stuffing side up, in a small flat baking dish. Bake for 15 minutes.

*Makes 8 servings.*

*This recipe may be used for mild sodium-restricted diets only. Those restricted to 1000-, 500-, or 250-mg. low-sodium diets must omit this recipe.*

# Spinach

**1 package (10 ounces) frozen chopped spinach or 1 pound fresh spinach, washed, cleaned, and cut up**
**1 tablespoon chopped onion**
**¼ teaspoon ground nutmeg**
**⅛ teaspoon white pepper**
**2 tablespoons unsalted butter or margarine**

Place spinach in a saucepan with ½ inch of water covering bottom of pan. Add onion, nutmeg, and pepper. Cook, covered, until tender. Drain well. Stir in butter until melted.

*Makes 4 servings.*

# Yellow Squash with Orange-Dill Sauce

**2 pounds summer crookneck or yellow squash**
**¼ cup unsalted butter or margarine**
**2 tablespoons undiluted frozen orange juice concentrate, thawed**
**1 small onion, thinly sliced**
**1 teaspoon sugar**
**1 teaspoon chopped dillweed**

Wash squash. Cut off a slice from the stem and blossom ends but do not pare. Cut into ½-inch slices. Melt butter in a skillet; stir in orange concentrate. Add squash and onion. Sprinkle with sugar and dill. Cook, covered, over moderate heat for 10 to 15 minutes or until squash is tender.

*Makes 4 to 6 servings.*

# Zucchini

**2 large zucchini**
**3 fresh tomatoes, cut up**
**1 sliced onion**
**¼ teaspoon white pepper**
**¼ teaspoon thyme**

Wash zucchini and cut into ¼-inch-thick circles. Place in a saucepan. Add an inch of water to pan. Add tomatoes and onion. Then add the pepper and thyme. Simmer covered about 10 minutes or until tender. Drain and serve.

*Makes 4 to 6 servings.*

# Zucchini and Mushrooms

**2 small zucchini, thinly sliced**
**½ pound sliced fresh mushrooms**
**2 tablespoons olive oil**
**¼ teaspoon thyme**
**⅛ teaspoon white pepper**

Place the zucchini and mushroom slices in a heavy skillet. Add olive oil and sauté vegetables until limp and tender. Stir in thyme and pepper.

*Makes 4 servings.*

## Ratatouille

¼ cup olive oil
1 large sliced onion
1 minced garlic clove
1 peeled and diced eggplant
1 zucchini, cut in ¼-inch slices
3 tomatoes, cut in wedges
2 green peppers, seeded and cut in strips
¼ teaspoon oregano
⅛ teaspoon pepper

Heat olive oil in a heavy skillet; sauté onion and garlic until onion is golden and translucent. Add eggplant, zucchini, tomatoes, and green peppers. Add oregano and pepper. Cover and simmer for 20 minutes, stirring occasionally.

*Makes 6 servings.*

## Mashed Yellow Turnips

1½ pounds yellow turnips, peeled and cut up
4 tablespoons unsalted butter or margarine
½ teaspoon grated lemon rind
¼ teaspoon mace
⅛ teaspoon pepper

Cook turnips in a small amount of water for about 20 minutes or until soft. Drain and mash. Add butter, lemon rind, mace, and pepper, whipping well together.

*Makes 4 to 6 servings.*

*This recipe may be used for all sodium-restricted diets, but those restricted to 1000-, 500-, or 250-mg. low-sodium diets should substitute low-sodium bread crumbs for regular bread crumbs and omit the Parmesan cheese.*

# Baked Stuffed Tomatoes

6 large tomatoes
1 cup bread crumbs
2 tablespoons chopped parsley
1 tablespoon minced onion
1 slightly beaten egg
1 tablespoon unsalted butter or margarine
2 tablespoons Parmesan cheese

Preheat oven to 350° F. Cut off stem ends of tomatoes and carefully scoop out centers. Chop tomato pulp coarsely; add bread crumbs, parsley, and onion. Stir in egg. Arrange tomato cups in a baking dish. Fill tomato cups with the mixture. Dot tops with butter and sprinkle with Parmesan cheese. Bake for about 30 minutes.

*Makes 6 servings.*

# Broiled Tomatoes

2 large tomatoes, cut in half
½ teaspoon crushed basil
⅛ teaspoon white pepper
1 tablespoon unsalted butter or margarine

Place tomato halves, cut side up, in a small broiling pan. Sprinkle top with crushed basil and pepper. Dot with butter. Slip under the broiler for 4 to 5 minutes. Serve at once.

*Makes 4 servings.*

# Herb-Roasted Corn

4 ears of corn
4 teaspoons unsalted butter or margarine
⅛ teaspoon pepper
½ teaspoon marjoram
½ teaspoon sugar

Remove husks and silk from ears of corn. Place each ear on a double square of aluminum foil. Dot with butter, and sprinkle with pepper, marjoram, and sugar. Wrap tightly. Roast in a 350° F. oven for 20 to 25 minutes, or roast outdoors on a rack over an open fire. Turn several times during roasting.

*Makes 4 servings.*

# Dilled Potatoes

6 potatoes, peeled and quartered
2 cups water
2 sprigs dillweed, cut up
2 tablespoons unsalted butter or margarine

Place potatoes, water, and dillweed in a saucepan; cook over low heat until tender (about 20 minutes). Drain off the water, leaving dill clinging to the potatoes. Toss with butter. Serve hot.

*Makes 6 to 8 servings.*

# Mashed Potato Casserole

6 medium potatoes, peeled and quartered
2 cups water
1 sliced onion
1 slightly beaten egg
2 tablespoons unsalted butter or margarine
1 tablespoon chopped chives
½ teaspoon paprika

Place potatoes, water, and sliced onion in a saucepan; cook about 20 minutes or until tender. Drain. Whip with a whisk or electric beater. Add egg and butter. Beat until fluffy. Grease a casserole dish with unsalted butter or margarine and spoon the whipped potato mixture into it. Sprinkle with chives and paprika. Bake in a 350° F. oven for 20 minutes.

*Makes 6 servings.*

# Baked Potato Puffs

4 large baking potatoes
1 slightly beaten egg
⅛ teaspoon white pepper
2 tablespoons unsalted butter or margarine
3 tablespoons grated low-sodium cheddar cheese

Bake potatoes in a 350° F. oven for 1 hour or until tender. Remove from oven. Cut each potato in half horizontally. Scoop out potato and reserve the shells. Mash potatoes; add egg, pepper, and butter. Beat until fluffy. Spoon back into the shells. Top with a sprinkling of grated cheddar cheese. Return to oven for 15 minutes or until heated through.

*Makes 8 servings.*

*This recipe may be prepared for all low-sodium diets, but those restricted to 1000-, 500-, or 250-mg. low-sodium diets should omit the carrots.*

# Potato-Prune Casserole

4 sweet potatoes
4 white potatoes
3 carrots, scraped and cut into 1-inch chunks
1 jar (16 ounces) prunes, pitted and drained
2 tablespoons unsalted butter or margarine
1 teaspoon sugar
¼ teaspoon nutmeg
⅛ teaspoon pepper
¾ cup orange juice

Preheat oven to 325° F. Peel and quarter potatoes; place in a heavy saucepan and cover with water. Add carrots. Cook until vegetables are almost soft. Drain. Empty potatoes and carrots into a 2-quart casserole. Melt butter in a small saucepan; stir in sugar, nutmeg, pepper, and orange juice. Pour over the potatoes and carrots. Bake for 30 minutes.

*Makes 8 to 10 servings.*

# Mashed Yams

4 large yams
2 tablespoons unsalted butter or margarine
1 tablespoon brown sugar
2 tablespoons finely grated orange rind

Preheat oven to 350° F. Peel yams and cut in quarters. Place in a heavy saucepan, cover with water, and bring to a boil. Reduce heat and simmer, covered, until yams are fork tender. Drain. Mash and add butter, brown sugar, and grated orange rind. Pile into a small casserole that has been greased with unsalted butter or margarine and bake for 15 minutes.

*Makes 6 servings.*

# Herbed Rice

¾ cup chopped onion
¼ cup unsalted butter or margarine
1 cup uncooked rice
2 cups water
½ teaspoon rosemary
½ teaspoon marjoram
½ teaspoon thyme

Sauté onion in butter in a saucepan until tender. Add rice, water, rosemary, marjoram, and thyme. Bring to a boil, stirring once. Cover and simmer for 14 minutes or until tender. Fluff and serve hot.

*Makes 6 servings.*

# Almond-Rice Peaches

8 large canned peach halves
1 cup cooked rice
2 tablespoons brown sugar
⅛ teaspoon cinnamon
2 tablespoons slivered unsalted almonds
1 tablespoon unsalted butter or margarine

Drain peach halves. Place rounded side down on a baking sheet. Combine rice with brown sugar and cinnamon. Mound in peach cavities. Insert slivered almonds into rice. Dot with butter and place in the broiler about 5 minutes.

*Makes 8 servings.*

# Baked Orange Rice

**1 cup uncooked rice**
**3 tablespoons unsalted butter or margarine**
**½ cup chopped green pepper**
**¼ cup chopped onion**
**2½ cups orange juice**

In a large heavy skillet toast rice over medium heat, shaking occasionally, for 20 minutes or until golden brown. Place in a 1-quart covered casserole. Meanwhile, in a small saucepan melt butter; add green pepper and onion and sauté for 5 minutes. Add the green pepper, onion, and the orange juice to casserole. Cover and bake, stirring occasionally, in a preheated 350° F. oven for 1 hour or until rice is tender and orange juice is absorbed.

*Makes 6 servings.*

# Spanish Rice

**1 cup enriched instant rice**
**1½ cups water**
**1 tablespoon unsalted butter or margarine**
**1 cup low-sodium canned tomatoes**
**1 chopped green pepper**
**1 chopped onion**
**¼ teaspoon chili powder**

Place rice, 1 cup of water, and butter in a saucepan; bring to a boil. Stir, cover, and remove from heat. Meanwhile, place tomatoes, green pepper, onion, and ½ cup water in an electric blender and mix. Pour tomato mixture into a saucepan, add chili powder, and heat for ten minutes. Pour over rice, mix, and fluff.

*Makes 4 servings.*

# 11

# Salt-Free Salad Dressings and Sauces

W HILE a simple oil and vinegar dressing might do the trick on salad greens, one does get tired of the same old tastes day after day. Here are a number of recipes that will be a refreshing change of pace.

Low-sodium-restricted patients should not use regular salad dressings unless they state that they are low-sodium dietetic dressings. And these are usually not as pleasant tasting as those you could prepare at home. An electric blender will be most helpful in making salt-free mayonnaise, bearnaise, and hollandaise sauces. If your blender has small jars, you will be able to blend and keep several kinds of dressings in the refrigerator at all times.

Check the vegetable recipes for those raw vegetables that should be eliminated from the low-sodium-restricted diet, and use your imagination to combine raw vegetables with your salad greens. Try some slivered cabbage, red onion, raw cauliflower, raw peas, raw mushrooms, and thinly sliced green and red peppers to give zest to your lettuce, chicory, endive, and escarole. It will all help you to have a happy dieter.

# French Dressing

⅔ cup salad oil
⅓ cup vinegar
¼ teaspoon dry mustard
¼ teaspoon paprika
⅛ teaspoon pepper

Combine all ingredients in a cruet and shake well. Store, covered, in refrigerator until ready to use. Shake well before using.

*Makes 1 cup dressing.*


# Italian Dressing

¾ cup salad oil
¼ cup vinegar
¼ cup water
1 minced garlic clove
¼ teaspoon cayenne
¼ teaspoon dry mustard
½ teaspoon sugar

Combine oil, vinegar, water, garlic, cayenne, mustard, and sugar in a cruet. Shake well. Store in the refrigerator until ready to serve.

*Makes about 1¼ cups.*

# Herb Dressing

⅔ cup salad oil
⅓ cup tarragon vinegar
½ minced garlic clove
⅛ teaspoon pepper
⅛ teaspoon thyme

Combine oil and vinegar in a cruet and shake well. Add garlic, pepper, and thyme. Store, covered, in refrigerator until ready to use. Shake well before using.

*Makes 1 cup dressing.*

# Spring Dressing

⅔ cup wine vinegar
⅓ cup water
1 tablespoon sugar
¼ teaspoon pepper
2 tablespoons finely chopped parsley
2 tablespoons salad oil

Stir together vinegar and water. Add sugar, pepper, and parsley. Just before serving, stir in salad oil.

*Makes 1¼ cups salad dressing.*

## Lemon Dressing

1 cup peanut oil
½ cup lemon juice
4 teaspoons sugar
2 tablespoons chopped parsley

Combine peanut oil and lemon juice. Add sugar and chopped parsley. Mix well.

*Makes about 1⅔ cups dressing.*

*This recipe may be used for all sodium-restricted diets, but those restricted to 500- and 250-mg. low-sodium diets should substitute low-sodium milk for regular milk.*

## Blender Remoulade Sauce

1 cup blender mayonnaise (see index)
2 tablespoons milk
2 tablespoons chopped parsley
1 teaspoon tarragon
1 teaspoon chervil
½ fresh cucumber, peeled and cut up

Prepare mayonnaise in electric blender. Add milk, parsley, tarragon, chervil, and cucumber. Blend together.

*Makes about 1¼ cups sauce.*

*This recipe may be used for all sodium-restricted diets, but those restricted to 500- and 250-mg. low-sodium diets should substitute low-sodium milk for regular milk.*

## Cooked Tarragon Salad Dressing

**2 tablespoons cornstarch**
**1 teaspoon dry mustard**
**¼ teaspoon paprika**
**⅛ teaspoon white pepper**
**1 cup milk**
**¼ cup unsalted butter or margarine**
**2 tablespoons tarragon vinegar**

Combine cornstarch, mustard, paprika, and pepper in a saucepan. Slowly stir in milk. Bring to a boil, stirring constantly, and boil for 2 minutes. Add butter; cook 2 minutes longer, stirring constantly. Remove from heat. Beat in vinegar with a rotary beater. Cool. Before serving, beat again until creamy.

*Makes about 1½ cups dressing.*

## Blender Hollandaise Sauce

**3 egg yolks**
**1 tablespoon lemon juice**
  **Dash of cayenne**
**¼ pound melted unsalted butter or margarine**

Blend egg yolks, lemon juice, and cayenne together in an electric blender with cover on. Remove cover; drizzle in a stream of melted butter while blender is turned on to medium speed. Turn blender off as the last of the butter is absorbed. This mixture may be refrigerated for up to two days in a tightly covered container. To heat, warm over simmering water.

*Makes about ¾ cup sauce.*

# Blender Béarnaise Sauce

2 tablespoons dry white wine
2 tablespoons tarragon vinegar
3 sprigs parsley
1 small onion, quartered
½ teaspoon tarragon
½ teaspoon chervil
⅛ teaspoon pepper
¾ cup blender hollandaise sauce (see index)

Combine in an electric blender the wine, vinegar, parsley, onion, tarragon, chervil, and pepper; process to grate parsley and onion. Empty mixture into a saucepan and cook until liquid is almost evaporated. Meanwhile, prepare hollandaise sauce in the electric blender; add cooked mixture to the hollandaise sauce and blend an instant more.

*Makes about 1 cup of sauce.*

# Blender Mayonnaise

1 egg
½ teaspoon dry mustard
½ teaspoon paprika
1 tablespoon vinegar
1 tablespoon lemon juice
1 cup salad oil

Put the egg, mustard, paprika, vinegar, lemon juice, and ¼ cup of salad oil into an electric blender; cover and process. Remove cover and pour remaining oil in a steady stream until all is absorbed. Turn machine off at once.

*Makes about 1¼ cups dressing.*

# 12

# Salt-Free Breads

W HILE those on a mild sodium-restricted diet may be able to eat regular breads and rolls without extra salt on top, others on a 1000-, 500-, or 250-mg. low-sodium-restricted diet have to eat low-sodium breads. Each regular slice of rye bread has about 135 mg. of sodium and each slice of white and whole-wheat bread has about 135 mg. of sodium. Several slices can add up to a lot of sodium, as you can see.

Low-sodium bakery products are available commercially, but this chapter will show you how easy it will be to bake your own breads and freeze the extras for another time. Many are raised with yeast and others have low-sodium baking powder. Yeast baking takes a little more time, but you do not have to stay in the kitchen during the entire preparation time. Merely set a timer, return to turn it off, and continue with the next steps. Some of the recipes have a newer refrigerator rising method and you might prefer to try those first because the timing does not have to be as accurate as the room-temperature rising method.

When marketing for commercial grain products, avoid those made with salt or monosodium glutamate. This includes all convenience-food bread and muffin mixes, quick-cooking cereals that contain a sodium compound, all dry cereals that have more than 6 milligrams of sodium to each 100 grams of cereal, self-rising flour, self-rising cornmeal, salted crackers, salted melba toast, frozen pancakes, and frozen waffles.

Grains you may use are regular flour, farina, grits, oatmeal, rolled wheat, wheat meal. Dry cereals that are low in sodium are puffed rice, puffed wheat and shredded wheat.

If you have the kind of patient who is fond of sandwiches or cannot eat a meal without a slice or two of bread, you will be particularly pleased to be able to offer breads that you know are low in sodium and tasty, too.

# White Bread

7¾ to 8¾ cups unsifted flour
3 tablespoons sugar
3 packages active dry yeast
⅓ cup softened unsalted butter or margarine
2⅔ cups very warm water
  Peanut oil

In a large bowl thoroughly mix 3 cups flour, sugar, and undissolved yeast. Add butter. Gradually add warm water to dry ingredients and beat with an electric mixer 2 minutes at medium speed, scraping the bowl occasionally. Add ½ cup flour. Beat at high speed 2 minutes, scraping bowl occasionally. Stir in enough additional flour to make a stiff dough. Turn out onto a lightly floured breadboard; knead until smooth and elastic (about 10 to 12 minutes). Cover with plastic wrap, then a towel. Let rest 20 minutes. Divide dough in half. Roll each half into a 9-by-14-inch rectangle. Shape into loaves by rolling the upper short side towards you. Seal with thumbs. Seal ends; fold sealed ends under. Be careful not to tear the dough. Grease two 9-by-5-by 3-inch loaf pans with unsalted butter or margarine. Place the loaves in the pans seam side down. Brush with peanut oil. Cover loosely with plastic wrap. Refrigerate 2 to 24 hours. When ready to bake, remove from refrigerator and uncover dough carefully. Let stand at room temperature 10 minutes. Puncture any gas bubbles which may have formed with a greased toothpick or metal skewer. Bake in a 400° F. oven for 35 to 40 minutes or until done. Remove from baking pans and cool on wire racks. Loaves may be frozen for future use.

*Makes 2 loaves.*

*This recipe may be used for all low-sodium diets, but those restricted to 500- or 250-mg. low-sodium diets should substitute low-sodium milk for regular milk.*

# Cinnamon Bread

**6½ to 7½ cups unsifted flour**
**⅓ and ½ cup sugar**
**2 packages active dry yeast**
**1 cup milk**
**¾ cup water**
**⅓ cup unsalted butter or margarine, plus 2 tablespoons melted unsalted butter or margarine**
**3 eggs, at room temperature, plus 1 slightly beaten egg white**
**2 teaspoons ground cinnamon**

In a large bowl thoroughly mix 2 cups flour, ⅓ cup sugar, and undissolved yeast. Combine milk, water, and ⅓ cup margarine in a saucepan. Heat over low heat until liquids are very warm, but margarine need not be melted. Gradually add to dry ingredients and beat 2 minutes at medium speed of electric mixer, scraping bowl occasionally. Add 3 whole eggs and ½ cup flour. Beat at high speed 2 minutes, scraping bowl occasionally. Stir in enough additional flour to make a stiff dough. Turn out onto a lightly floured breadboard; knead until smooth and elastic (about 8 to 10 minutes). Place in a bowl that has been well greased with unsalted butter or margarine, turning to grease all sides. Cover; let rise in a warm place, free from drafts, until doubled in size (about 35 minutes). Combine ½ cup sugar and cinnamon. Punch dough down; divide in half. Roll each half into a 9-by-14 inch rectangle. Brush lightly with 2 tablespoons melted margarine. Sprinkle each with half the cinnamon and sugar mixture. Beginning at the 9-inch end, tightly roll dough like a jelly roll and shape into loaves. Grease two 9-by-5-by-3-inch loaf pans with unsalted butter or margarine. Tuck ends of the loaves under and place them seam side down into the loaf pans. Cover; let rise in a warm place, free from drafts, until doubled in size (about 35 minutes). Brush with egg white. Bake on lowest rack in a 375° F. oven for 45 minutes, or until golden brown. Remove from pan and cool on wire racks. Loaves may be frozen for future use.

*Makes 2 loaves.*

*This recipe may be used for all low-sodium diets, but those restricted to 500- or 250-mg. low-sodium diets should substitute low-sodium milk for regular milk.*

## Oatmeal Bread

½ cup warm water
2 packages active dry yeast
1¾ cups warm milk
¼ cup firmly packed brown sugar
3 tablespoons unsalted butter or margarine
5 to 6 cups unsifted flour
1 cup quick rolled oats
  Peanut oil

Measure warm water into a large warm bowl. Sprinkle in yeast; stir until dissolved. Add warm milk, brown sugar, and margarine. Add 2 cups flour. Beat with rotary beater for 1 minute or until smooth. Add 1 cup flour and the oats. Beat vigorously with a wooden spoon until smooth. Add enough additional flour to make a soft dough. Turn out onto a lightly floured breadboard and knead until smooth and elastic (about 8 to 10 minutes). Cover with plastic wrap, then a towel. Let rest 20 minutes. Divide dough in half. Roll each half into a 8-by-12-inch rectangle. Beginning with the upper short side, roll towards you. Seal with thumbs. Seal ends; fold sealed ends under. Be careful not to tear the dough. Grease two pans, 8½-by-4½-by-2½-inches each with unsalted butter or margarine. Place the loaves seam side down in the pans. Brush loaves with peanut oil. Cover pans loosely with plastic wrap. Refrigerate 2 to 24 hours. When ready to bake, remove from refrigerator. Uncover dough carefully; let stand uncovered 10 minutes at room temperature. Puncture any gas bubbles that may have formed with a greased toothpick or metal skewer. Bake at 400° F. for 30 to 40 minutes or until done. Loaves may be frozen for future use.

*Makes 2 loaves.*

*This recipe may be used for all low-sodium diets, but those restricted to 500- or 250-mg. low-sodium diets should substitute low-sodium milk for regular milk.*

## Tiny Herb Loaves

½ cup milk
3 tablespoons sugar
3 tablespoons unsalted butter or margarine
1½ cups warm water
1 package active dry yeast
5½ to 6½ cups unsifted flour
1 cup chopped chives
1 cup chopped parsley
¼ cup melted unsalted butter or margarine

Scald milk; stir in sugar and butter. Let stand until lukewarm. Measure warm water into a large warm bowl. Sprinkle yeast over water and stir until dissolved. Add lukewarm milk mixture and 3 cups of flour. Beat until smooth. Stir in enough additional flour to form a stiff dough. Turn out onto a lightly floured breadboard; knead until smooth and elastic (about 8 to 10 minutes). Grease a bowl with unsalted butter or margarine and place the dough in it, turning to grease all sides. Cover; let rise in a warm place, free from drafts, until doubled in size (about 1 hour). Combine chives and parsley. Punch down dough; turn out onto breadboard. Cover; let rest 15 minutes. Divide dough into 6 equal pieces. Roll each piece into a 8-by-12-inch rectangle; brush with melted butter and sprinkle with herb mixture. Roll up tightly, like a jelly roll, to make a 12-inch-long roll; pinch seams to seal. Repeat until each piece is rolled in this way. Grease baking sheets with unsalted butter or margarine and place the rolls on them about 2 inches apart. Cover; let rise in a warm place, free from drafts, until doubled in size, (about 1 hour). Bake at 375° F. 15 to 20 minutes or until done. Loaves may be frozen.

*Makes 6 loaves.*

*This recipe may be used for all low-sodium diets, but those restricted to 500- or 250-mg. low-sodium diets should substitute low-sodium milk for regular milk.*

# Swedish Rye Bread

3½ to 4 cups unsifted white flour
1½ cups unsifted rye flour
⅓ cup firmly packed dark brown sugar
1 teaspoon caraway seed
2 packages active dry yeast
1 cup milk
1 cup water
2 tablespoons unsalted butter or margarine

Combine flours. In a large bowl thoroughly mix 1½ cups of the mixed flours with brown sugar, caraway seed, and undissolved yeast. Combine milk, water, and butter in a saucepan. Heat over low heat until liquids are very warm (butter does not need to be melted). Gradually add to dry ingredients and beat for 2 minutes at medium speed of electric mixer, scraping bowl occasionally. Add ¾ cup flour mixture. Beat at high speed for 2 minutes, scraping bowl occasionally. Stir in enough additional flour mixture to make a stiff dough. (If necessary use additional white flour to obtain desired consistency.) Cover; let rise in a warm place, free from drafts, until doubled in size (about 40 minutes). Punch dough down. Cover; let rise again until doubled in size (about 20 minutes). Punch down again. Turn into a 1½-quart casserole that has been well greased with unsalted butter or margarine. Bake at 400° F. about 40 minutes or until done. Remove from casserole and cool on a wire rack.

*Makes 1 round loaf.*

*This recipe may be used for all low sodium-restricted diets, but those restricted to 500- or 250-mg. low-sodium diets should substitute low-sodium milk for regular milk.*

# Prune Bread

3 cups flour
3½ teaspoons low-sodium baking powder
1 cup chopped pitted prunes
1 teaspoon nutmeg
¾ cup sugar
1 egg
1½ cups milk
2 tablespoons salad oil

Preheat oven to 350° F. Combine flour, baking powder, prunes, nutmeg, and sugar. Beat egg, milk, and salad oil together; stir all at once into dry ingredients. Grease a 9 -by-5-by-3-inch loaf pan with unsalted butter or margarine. Pour the mixture into it and bake for 1 hour or until brown and firm to the touch. Unmold and cool thoroughly before slicing.

*Makes 12 servings.*

# Orange-Peanut Butter Bread

½ cup low-sodium peanut butter
2 tablespoons salad oil
1⅓ cups orange juice
1 egg
¾ cup sugar
2 cups sifted flour
1 tablespoon low-sodium baking powder
1 tablespoon grated orange rind

Preheat oven to 350° F. Beat peanut butter until fluffy. Gradually add salad oil and orange juice, beating until smooth. Beat in egg and sugar. Sift together flour and baking powder; stir into peanut butter mixture, blending well. Stir in orange rind. Grease loaf pans with unsalted butter or margarine. Turn into two 3-by-7-by-2-inch loaf pans and bake for 1 hour, or turn into one 9-by-5-by-3-inch loaf pan and bake for 1 hour 15 minutes.

*Makes 1 large or 2 small loaves.*

# Poppyseed Rolls

1½ cups warm water
1 package active dry yeast
2 tablespoons sugar
6 tablespoons softened unsalted butter or margarine plus
  1 tablespoon melted unsalted butter or margarine
4 cups unsifted flour
2 teaspoons poppyseeds

Pour warm water into a large bowl. Sprinkle yeast over water and stir until dissolved. Add sugar, 6 tablespoons softened butter, and 2 cups flour. Beat until butter is blended in. Stir in remaining 2 cups flour to make a soft dough. Turn out on a lightly floured breadboard; knead until smooth and elastic (about 10 minutes). Grease a bowl with unsalted butter or margarine. Place the dough in the bowl, turning to grease on all sides. Cover. Let rise in a warm place, free from drafts, until doubled in size (about 30 minutes). Punch down and turn out on a lightly floured breadboard. Divide dough in half. Form each half into a long roll and cut each roll into 12 equal pieces. Form each piece of dough into a smooth ball. Grease two 9-inch-round cake pans with unsalted butter or margarine. Place 12 such rolls in each pan. Cover. Let rise in warm place, free from draft, until doubled in size again (about 45 minutes). Lightly brush rolls with melted butter. Sprinkle with poppyseeds. Bake in a 375°F. oven for 25 to 30 minutes or until lightly browned. Excess rolls may be frozen for future use.

*Makes 2 dozen rolls.*

# Hamburger Buns

**5¾ to 6¾ cups unsifted flour**
**⅓ cup instant nonfat dry milk solids**
**¼ cup sugar**
**2 packages active dry yeast**
**⅓ cup softened unsalted butter or margarine**
**2 cups warm water**

In a large bowl thoroughly mix 2 cups of the flour, dry milk solids, sugar, and undissolved yeast. Add butter. Gradually add warm water to dry ingredients and beat 2 minutes at medium speed of an electric mixer, scraping bowl occasionally. Add ¾ cup flour. Beat at high speed 2 minutes, scraping bowl occasionally. Stir in enough additional flour to make a stiff dough. Turn out onto a lightly floured breadboard; knead until smooth and elastic (about 8 to 10 minutes). Place in a bowl that has been greased with unsalted butter or margarine, turning to grease all sides. Cover; let rise in a warm place, free from drafts, until doubled in size (about 45 minutes). Punch dough down; let rise again until less than doubled (about 20 minutes). Divide dough in half; cut each half into 10 equal pieces. Form each piece into a smooth round ball. Grease baking sheets with unsalted butter or margarine and place the buns on them about 2 inches apart; press to flatten. Cover; let rise in a warm place, free from drafts, until doubled in size (about 1 hour). Bake in a 375° F. oven for 15 to 20 minutes or until done. Remove from baking sheets and cool on wire racks. Extra buns may be frozen for future use.

*Makes 20 buns.*

*This recipe may be used for all low-sodium diets, but those restricted to 500- or 250-mg. low-sodium diets should substitute low-sodium milk for regular milk.*

# Wheat Germ Popovers

¾ cup unsifted all-purpose flour
¼ cup wheat germ
1 teaspoon dried parsley
3 large eggs
1 cup milk
2 tablespoons unsalted butter or margarine,
  melted strawberry preserves

Preheat oven to 400° F. Generously grease (using unsalted butter or margarine) five 6-ounce ovenproof glass custard cups; place on a baking sheet. Combine flour, wheat germ, and parsley. In a medium-sized bowl, beat eggs until frothy. Add milk and butter. Gradually add flour mixture, beating until batter is smooth and blended (about 2 minutes). Pour batter into custard cups, filling them to within ¾ inch of the tops, stirring batter to distribute wheat germ evenly. Bake for 1 hour without opening oven door. Then pull out oven rack and quickly make a small slit in the top of each popover to let out steam. Return to oven and bake 5 minutes longer or until tops are crisp and golden brown. Remove popovers from cups and serve hot with strawberry preserves.

*Makes 5 servings.*

*This recipe may be used for all low-sodium diets, but those restricted to 500- or 250-mg. low-sodium diets should substitute low-sodium milk for regular milk.*

## Marmalade Sticky Buns

1 cup milk
¼ cup sugar
1 cup plus 3 tablespoons unsalted butter or margarine
½ cup warm water
2 packages active dry yeast
2 eggs
5 to 5½ cups unsifted flour
1¾ cups orange marmalade
1 cup finely chopped unsalted walnuts
¾ teaspoon ground cinnamon

Scald milk; stir in sugar and 1 cup butter. Let stand until lukewarm. Measure warm water into a large warm bowl. Sprinkle in yeast; stir until dissolved. Add lukewarm milk mixture. Add eggs and 3 cups flour; beat until smooth. Stir in enough additional flour (2 to 2½ cups) to make a stiff dough. Cover with a towel. Let stand at room temperature 20 minutes. Meanwhile, combine marmalade and 3 tablespoons butter in a saucepan; heat and stir until well blended. Grease 36 small muffin cups (1¼ inches across the top) and a 9-inch square pan with unsalted butter or margarine. Place ½ teaspoon of this marmalade mixture into each cup and pour remaining marmalade mixture into the square pan. Turn dough out onto a floured breadboard. With floured hands, knead slightly (about 15 turns). Form dough into a ball and divide in half. Refrigerate one half and divide the other half in two again. Roll each piece into an 8-by-18 inch rectangle. Spread each with marmalade; sprinkle evenly with ⅓ cup of a combined walnut and cinnamon mixture. Roll each from the long side, like a jelly roll, to form a roll 18 inches long. Pinch the seam of each to seal. Mark each roll for 18 slices and cut. Place slices in prepared muffin tins.

Remove remaining dough from refrigerator. Roll into a 9-by-14 inch rectangle. Spread with remaining marmalade mixture and sprinkle evenly with remaining nut mixture. Roll from the short side, like a jelly roll, to form a roll 9 inches long. Pinch seam to seal. Cut into 9 slices. Place in the 9-inch-square pan with rolls touching each other. Cover all rolls loosely with waxed paper brushed with oil, then top with plastic wrap. Refrigerate for 2 to 24 hours. When ready to bake, uncover dough and let stand at room temperature for 10 minutes. Bake small rolls in a 375° F. oven for 15 to 20 minutes or until light golden brown. Bake larger rolls 30 minutes or until done. Invert immediately onto wire racks; spoon any topping that remains in pans onto rolls. Serve warm. Rolls may be frozen for future use, and then warmed in the oven before serving.

*Makes 3 dozen small and 9 large rolls.*

*This recipe may be used by those restricted to a mild-sodium diet. Those restricted to 1000-, 500-, or 250-mg. low-sodium diet should omit this recipe.*

# Cornmeal Griddle Cakes

**2 eggs**
**1¼ cups buttermilk**
**1 tablespoon salad oil**
**1 cup yellow cornmeal**
**1 teaspoon sugar**
  **Raspberry, apricot, or boysenberry fruit syrup**

Beat eggs until frothy. Add buttermilk, oil, cornmeal, and sugar. Stir only until dry ingredients are moistened. Lightly grease a griddle with unsalted butter or margarine. Then pour 2 tablespoons of batter for each pancake onto the hot griddle. Cook until edges are crisp. Turn and cook until underside is golden brown. Serve hot with a pitcher of fruit syrup.

*Makes 18 griddle cakes (approximately 3 inches each.)*

# 13

# Salt-Free Desserts

Iᴛ is bad enough to be on a sodium-restricted regime, but when it affects your sweet tooth, it's unfair. And it does limit your cravings unless someone will take the time to bake these delectable cakes, cookies, and pies.

You may ask, "But what about baking powder and baking soda?" There are substitutes that do a fine job and are available at certain specialty food stores. Or they may be prepared by your pharmacist. One word of caution: If the patient is also on a low-potassium diet there may be a problem with these substitutes because they are based on potassium bicarbonate and potassium bitartrate. If you have a go-ahead from the doctor, ask the pharmacist for a low-sodium baking powder made from potassium bicarbonate, cornstarch, tartaric acid, and potassium bitartrate. You may also purchase potassium bicarbonate to use in place of baking soda. These may be substituted for the sodium ingredients in some of your favorite desserts, but be sure to check as to whether the baking powder amounts will have to be increased when you use the low-sodium substitute.

Be sure to read the labels on packages of dried and frozen fruit. Sodium sulfite is often added to dried fruit and salt is sometimes added to frozen fruit. Avoid any packages that have these additions.

All natural fruits and all canned fruits that are sodium-free may be used for desserts. However, if the patient is on a low-carbohydrate diet as well as a low-sodium diet, then you will have to use only water-packed fruits found in the dietetic canned food section of your food market.

Avoid the use of all convenience food mixes for cakes, puddings, and pies. Do not use frozen cookie dough or any frozen cakes or pies. Those restricted to a mild-sodium diet may have ice cream occasionally, those restricted to 1000-, 500-, or 250-mg. diets may not, unless it is a special low-sodium ice cream. Baking chocolate may be used, if it has no added sodium compound. Candy may be made at home, unless you find a shop that specializes in hand-dipped chocolates that will make a low-sodium candy for you.

Unflavored gelatin has no sodium. Read all other fruit gelatin boxes for amounts of sodium products included. Some are low enough for the mild-sodium-restricted diet and the 1000-mg. low-sodium diet, but not for the 500- or 250-mg. low-sodium diets.

This chapter is full of satisfying desserts to meet your needs. Even the crankiest patients will finish their meals with sweet content.

# Apricot Whip

2 cans (8 ounces each) juice-packed unsweetened apricot
  halves
1 envelope (4 servings) low-calorie orange gelatin
1 cup boiling water
1 tablespoon lemon juice
  Mint sprigs (optional)

Drain the juice from the apricots into a measuring cup;
add water to juice to make 1 cup. Finely chop or crush the
apricots and set aside. Dissolve gelatin in boiling water. Add
measured liquid and lemon juice. Place bowl of gelatin
inside a larger bowl of ice and cold water; stir until
thickened, then whip with a rotary beater or an electric
mixer until fluffy and thick and about double in volume.
Fold in apricots. Pour into 8 individual molds or dessert
dishes. Chill until firm (at least 2 hours). Unmold. Garnish
with mint sprigs, if desired.

*Makes 8 servings.*

# Lemon Snow

1 envelope (4 servings) low-calorie lemon gelatin
1 cup boiling water
1 cup cold water
2 teaspoons lemon juice
½ teaspoon grated lemon rind
2 egg whites

Dissolve gelatin in boiling water in a bowl. Add cold
water, lemon juice, and lemon rind. Chill until slightly
thickened. Then beat with a rotary beater or an electric
mixer until fluffy and thick and about double in volume.
Beat egg whites until they form soft rounded peaks; fold into
whipped gelatin. Pour into a 6-cup mold. Chill until firm
(about 4 hours). Unmold.

*Makes 8 servings.*

# Orange Frappé

**1 envelope (4 servings) low-calorie orange gelatin**
**½ cup boiling water**
**2 tablespoons orange juice**
**2½ cups crushed ice**

Place gelatin and boiling water in an electric blender; blend until gelatin is dissolved. Add orange juice and blend until mixture is fluffy. Add crushed ice and blend 3 to 4 minutes or until mixture is slightly thickened. Serve at once.

*Makes 8 servings.*

*This recipe may be used by those restricted to a mild-sodium diet. Those restricted to 1000-, 500-, or 250-mg. low-sodium diet should omit this recipe.*

# Orange Sherbet

**2 eggs**
**½ cup sugar**
**½ cup light corn syrup**
**2 cups buttermilk**
**1 can (6 ounce) undiluted frozen**
   **orange juice concentrate, thawed**
**¼ teaspoon grated orange rind**

Beat eggs in a large bowl. Slowly beat in sugar and then the corn syrup. Mix in buttermilk, orange juice concentrate, and orange rind. Pour into a metal pan or tray; place in the freezer. Freeze until almost firm (about 1 hour). Turn into a large mixing bowl; break up into small pieces and beat smooth. Return to freezer pan or serving dishes and freeze until firm (about 3 hours).

*Makes 1 quart sherbet.*

## Mousse au Chocolat

2 ounces baking chocolate
3 tablespoons sugar
3 tablespoons boiling water
1 teaspoon rum
2 eggs, separated

Grate chocolate and place in an electric blender; add sugar and boiling water. Blend. Add rum and egg yolks; blend again. Beat egg whites until stiff; fold chocolate mixture into stiff egg whites. Spoon into dessert dishes and chill until firm.

*Makes 4 servings.*

*This recipe may be used for all sodium-restricted diets, but those restricted to 500- or 250-mg. low-sodium diets should substitute low-sodium milk for regular milk.*

## Rum Custard

3 eggs
¼ cup sugar
2 cups milk, scalded
1 tablespoon rum extract
½ teaspoon nutmeg

Preheat oven to 350° F. Beat eggs slightly. Add sugar and mix well. Very slowly add the scalded milk, stirring constantly. Stir in the rum extract. Pour into custard cups and sprinkle with nutmeg. Place in a pan of hot water and bake for 30 to 35 minutes or until a knife inserted in the center of the custard comes out clean.

*Makes 4 servings.*

# Baked Apples

6 large baking apples
½ cup brown sugar
⅓ cup raisins
2 tablespoons grated orange peel
½ teaspoon cinnamon
2 tablespoons unsalted butter or margarine
1 cup boiling water

Preheat oven to 350° F. Wash and core apples. Place in a flat baking dish. Combine brown sugar, raisins, orange peel, and cinnamon. Fill cavity of each apple with this mixture. Dot with butter. Pour boiling water around apples. Bake, uncovered, for about 1 hour or until tender. Baste apples occasionally with pan liquid. Serve warm or cold.

*Makes 6 servings.*

# Ginger Pears

4 fresh pears, peeled, cored, and halved
1 cup water
1 tablespoon sugar
¼ teaspoon ground ginger

Arrange pears in a small saucepan. Pour water around them; add sugar and ginger. Cover and simmer for 20 minutes or until pears are tender. Serve hot or chilled.

*Makes 4 servings.*

# Poached Oranges

**6 oranges**
**3 tablespoons unsalted butter or margarine**
**¾ cup currant jelly**
**½ cup orange juice**
**1 tablespoon cornstarch**
**2 tablespoons cold water**

Remove thin outer rind from three of the oranges with a vegetable peeler and cut into very thin slivers. Place the rind in a small saucepan with water to cover; bring to a boil, reduce heat, and simmer for 10 minutes. Drain, reserving rind. Cut remaining peel and white membrane from all 6 oranges. Place a large skillet over low heat; add butter and jelly and stir until melted. Stir in orange juice and reserved cooked slivered rind. Add oranges and cook gently, spooning sauce over oranges, for about 5 minutes. Mix together cornstarch and water to form a smooth paste. Stir into the sauce in the skillet. Continue to stir over heat until sauce thickens. Continue spooning sauce over oranges until heated through (about 5 minutes longer). Serve warm, covered with sauce.

*Makes 6 servings.*

# Blueberry Pie

PIE CRUST:

**⅔ cup unsalted butter or margarine**
**2 cups sifted flour**
**4 to 6 tablespoons ice water**

Cut butter into flour with a pastry blender until pieces are the size of small peas. Slowly sprinkle in ice water, using just enough water to hold ingredients together. Blend well. Roll half the dough to fit a 9-inch pie pan.

FILLING:

**1 cup sugar**
**¼ cup flour**
**2 tablespoons lemon juice**
**¼ teaspoon cinnamon**
**¼ teaspoon nutmeg**
**3 cups fresh blueberries**
**1 tablespoon unsalted butter**

Combine sugar, flour, lemon juice, cinnamon, and nutmeg. Place half the berries in the pastry shell; sprinkle with half of the sugar mixture. Add remaining berries and sprinkle with remaining sugar mixture. Dot with 1 tablespoon butter. Roll remaining pie crust and top pie. Trim edges and crimp as desired. Bake in a 425° F. oven for 30 to 40 minutes.

*Makes 6 to 8 servings.*

*This recipe may be used for those restricted to a mild-sodium diet. Those restricted to 1000-, 500-, or 250-mg. low-sodium diets should omit this recipe.*

# Peach Meringue Pie

PIE CRUST:

¼ cup unsalted butter or margarine, melted
2 cups flaked coconut

Preheat oven to 300° F. Combine melted butter and coconut. Press evenly into an ungreased 9-inch pie pan. Bake for 30 to 35 minutes or until golden brown. Cool. Reset oven to 325° F.

FILLING:

2 eggs, separated
1 can (15 ounces) sweetened condensed milk
½ cup lemon juice
1½ cups finely chopped peaches, fresh, canned, or frozen
1 teaspoon lemon rind
¼ teaspoon almond extract
4 tablespoons sugar

Beat egg yolks. Blend in condensed milk. Gradually add lemon juice. Blend in peaches, lemon rind, and almond extract. Pour into cooled coconut crust. Beat egg whites until foamy throughout. Gradually add sugar, beating thoroughly after each addition. Continue beating until mixture forms stiff shiny peaks. Pile lightly on pie filling, carefully spreading to the edge of crust to seal. Bake at 325° F. until lightly browned (about 15 minutes). Cool.

*Makes 8 servings.*

*This recipe may be used for all low-sodium diets, but those restricted to 500- or 250-mg. low-sodium diets should substitute low-sodium milk for regular milk.*

# Upside-Down Apple Cake

2 tablespoons unsalted butter or margarine, melted
½ cup firmly packed light brown sugar
½ teaspoon cinnamon
2 cups peeled thinly sliced cooking apples
2 cups sifted flour
1 cup sugar
2½ teaspoons low-sodium baking powder
½ cup unsalted butter or margarine, softened
¾ cup milk
1 egg, beaten

Preheat oven to 375° F. Pour 2 tablespoons melted butter into a 9-inch-square baking pan. Mix brown sugar and cinnamon; sprinkle over butter. Arrange apple slices in rows in bottom of pan of butter mixture. Sift together the flour, sugar, and baking powder into a large bowl. Add 8 tablespoons butter and ½ cup milk; beat 2 minutes. Add remaining ¼ cup milk and the beaten egg; beat 2 additional minutes at medium speed. Spread batter over apples in pan. Bake in the preheated oven for 30 to 40 minutes. Cool in pan on a wire rack for 10 minutes. Invert onto a serving plate. Cut into squares and serve warm.

*Makes 9 squares.*

# Orange-Honey Date Cake

CAKE:

⅔ cup unsalted butter, margarine or vegetable shortening
¾ cup packed brown sugar
3 eggs
¾ cup honey
1 package (8 ounces) pitted dates, finely cut
2 tablespoons grated orange rind
3⅓ cups sifted flour
2½ teaspoons low-sodium baking powder
1½ teaspoons cinnamon
¾ teaspoon nutmeg
¼ teaspoon ginger
½ cup orange juice

Preheat oven to 350° F. Cream together butter and sugar. Add eggs, one at a time, beating after each addition. Gradually add honey; stir in dates and orange rind. Sift together flour, baking powder, cinnamon, nutmeg, and ginger. Blend into creamed mixture alternately with orange juice, beginning and ending with dry ingredients. Grease (using unsalted butter or margarine) and flour a 9-inch tube pan. Turn the batter into the pan and bake for 1 hour and 10 minutes, or until cake tester comes out clean. Cool 10 minutes and remove from pan; cool completely. Frost top of cake with orange glaze, if desired.

ORANGE GLAZE:

2 tablespoons orange juice
1½ cups confectioners' sugar

Stir the orange juice into the confectioners' sugar and mix well until smooth. Spread the glaze on the cake.

*Makes one 9-inch cake.*

*This recipe may be used by those restricted to a mild-sodium diet. Those restricted to a 1000-, 500-, or 250-mg. diet should omit this recipe.*

# Applesauce Cookies

1½ cups unsalted butter or margarine
2 cups firmly packed dark brown sugar
2 eggs
½ cup buttermilk
1½ cups applesauce
3½ cups sifted flour
1 teaspoon low-sodium baking powder
1 teaspoon nutmeg
1 teaspoon cinnamon
½ teaspoon ginger
1½ cups chopped unsalted walnuts

Preheat oven to 400° F. Cream together butter and sugar. Add eggs, one at a time, beating after each addition. Add buttermilk. Stir in applesauce. Sift together, flour, baking powder, nutmeg, cinnamon, and ginger. Add to creamed mixture. Add nuts. Chill 2 hours. Grease cookie sheets with unsalted butter or margarine. Drop the batter by teaspoonfuls onto the cookie sheets, about 3 inches apart. Bake 10 to 12 minutes or until edges are brown.

*Makes 7 dozen cookies.*

*This recipe may be used for all low-sodium diets, but those restricted to 500- or 250-mg. low-sodium diets should substitute low-sodium milk for regular milk.*

## Chocolate Nut Cake

2¼ cups sifted cake flour (not self-rising)
1 tablespoon low-sodium baking powder
½ cup unsalted butter or margarine
2 cups sugar
2 eggs
4 melted squares unsweetened baking chocolate
1½ cups milk
2 teaspoons vanilla
1 cup finely chopped unsalted nuts

Preheat oven to 375° F. Sift flour with baking powder. Cream butter; gradually add sugar, beating until light and fluffy. Add eggs, one at a time, beating thoroughly after each addition. Blend in melted chocolate. Then add the flour mixture alternately with milk, a small amount at a time, beating after each addition until smooth. Stir in vanilla and nuts. Pour into a 10-inch tube pan that has been lined on the bottom with waxed paper. Bake 55 to 60 minutes or until a cake tester inserted in center comes out clean. Cool in pan for 15 minutes; remove from pan and cool thoroughly on a rack.

*Makes 12 servings.*

*This recipe may be used by those restricted to a mild-sodium diet. Those restricted to 1000-, 500-, or 250-mg. low-sodium diets should omit this recipe.*

# Carrot Nut Cake

9 eggs, separated
1½ cups sugar
1½ cups flour
2 teaspoons cinnamon
½ cup undiluted frozen orange juice concentrate, thawed
1 tablespoon grated orange rind
1 cup shredded carrots (2 to 3 medium-sized carrots)
½ cup finely chopped unsalted walnuts
½ cup chopped raisins

Preheat oven to 325° F. In a large bowl, beat egg whites until foamy. Gradually beat in ½ cup of the sugar, continuing to beat until stiff peaks form. Set aside. In a large bowl, beat egg yolks until thick and lemon colored. Gradually beat in remaining 1 cup sugar. Add mixture of flour and cinnamon to beaten egg yolks, alternating with undiluted orange juice, and mix only until well blended. Stir in grated orange rind, shredded carrots, walnuts, and raisins. Fold egg yolk mixture gently into egg whites until batter is well blended, but do not overmix. Turn into an ungreased 10-inch tube pan. Bake 55 to 60 minutes or until cake is golden brown and springs back when touched lightly with a finger. Invert pan on cake rack or neck of a bottle until cake is completely cool. When cool, loosen cake from pan and turn out onto a cake plate.

*Makes one 10-inch cake.*

# Yeast Loaf Cake

¾ cup warm water
1 package active dry yeast
1 cup plus 1 tablespoon sugar
2¼ cups sifted cake flour (plain, not self-rising)
½ cup unsalted butter or margarine
2 eggs, beaten
1 teaspoon vanilla

Measure warm water into a large bowl. Sprinkle in yeast. Add 1 tablespoon sugar and stir until dissolved. Add 1 cup of the flour. Beat until smooth. Cover. Let rise in a warm place, free from drafts, until doubled in size (about 30 minutes). Cream butter thoroughly. Gradually add 1 cup sugar and beat well. Add to yeast mixture. Add beaten eggs, vanilla, and remaining flour. Beat until well blended. Grease well an 8-inch-square pan with unsalted butter or margarine. Pour the batter in the pan and cover. Let rise in a warm place, free from drafts, until doubled in size (about 1 hour). Bake in a 350° F. oven about 40 minutes or until done. Remove from pan and cool.

*Makes 12 servings.*

# Coffeecake

COFFECAKE:

**1 cup warm water**
**2 packages active dry yeast**
**4 cups unsifted flour**
**½ cup unsalted butter or margarine**
**½ cup sugar**
**2 eggs**
  **Streusel topping**

Pour warm water into a mixing bowl. Sprinkle in yeast and stir until dissolved. Stir in 1½ cups flour; beat until smooth. Cover; let rise in a warm place, free from drafts, until doubled in size (about 30 minutes). Cream butter, add sugar, and beat thoroughly. Add eggs and remaining flour to the margarine and sugar. Mix, making a soft dough and add to the raised dough. Turn out onto a lightly floured breadboard. Knead until smooth and elastic (about 5 minutes). Grease a bowl with unsalted butter or margarine. Place the dough in the bowl and turn to grease all sides. Cover; let rise in a warm place, free from drafts, until doubled in size (about 1 hour). Divide dough in thirds. Grease three 8-inch-square pans with unsalted butter or margarine. Press the dough into the pans and let rise in a warm place, free from drafts, until doubled in size (about 30 minutes). Sprinkle with streusel topping.

STREUSEL TOPPING:

**⅓ cup unsalted butter or margarine**
**⅓ cup sugar**
**1 cup unsifted flour**
**1 teaspoon cinnamon**

Cream butter or margarine. Add sugar gradually. Add flour and cinnamon; stir until well mixed and crumbly. Sprinkle over the coffeecake and bake at 400° F. for 20 minutes or until done.

*Makes three 8-inch cakes.*

*This recipe may be used for all low-sodium diets, but those restricted to 500- or 250- mg. low-sodium diets should substitute low-sodium milk for regular milk.*

# Lemon Wafers

1½ tablespoons unsalted butter, margarine, or shortening
½ cup sugar
1 egg
1 teaspoon lemon extract
¾ cup sifted flour
1 teaspoon low-sodium baking powder
3 tablespoons milk

Preheat oven to 350° F. Cream butter and sugar. Beat in egg and lemon extract. Sift together flour and baking powder. Add alternately with milk to sugar mixture, beating well. Grease a cookie sheet with unsalted butter or margarine. Drop by half teaspoonfuls about 2 inches apart onto the cookie sheet. Bake for 10 to 15 minutes or until wafers have a brown edge.

*Makes 2 dozen.*

# Brownies

1 cup semisweet chocolate morsels
⅓ cup unsalted butter, margarine, or shortening
½ cup sugar
2 eggs
1 teaspoon vanilla
½ cup sifted flour
½ teaspoon low-sodium baking powder
½ cup chopped unsalted nuts

Preheat oven to 375° F. Put semisweet chocolate morsels and butter in a saucepan. Place over low heat, stirring constantly, until melted. Remove from heat. Add sugar, mixing thoroughly. Add eggs, one at a time, beating well after each addition. Stir in vanilla. Sift together flour and baking powder; add to chocolate mixture and mix until blended. Stir in nuts. Grease an 8-inch-square pan with unsalted butter or margarine. Turn the batter into the pan and bake 25 to 30 minutes. Cool. Cut into 2-inch squares.

*Makes 16 squares.*

*This recipe may be used for all low-sodium diets, but those restricted to 500- or 250-mg. low-sodium diets should substitute low-sodium milk for regular milk.*

# Date Bars

½ cup unsalted butter or margarine
1½ cups packed brown sugar
2 teaspoons vanilla extract
2 eggs
2 cups sifted flour
1 teaspoon low-sodium baking powder
½ teaspoon pumpkin pie spice
¼ cup milk
2 cups chopped pitted dates

Preheat oven to 375° F. Cream together butter, sugar, and vanilla. Beat in eggs. Sift together flour, baking powder, and pumpkin pie spice; add to creamed mixture alternately with milk. Mix in dates. Grease a jelly roll pan with unsalted butter or margarine. Spread the batter in the pan and bake for 20 to 25 minutes. Cool and cut into bars.

*Makes about 3 dozen bars.*

*This recipe may be used for all low-sodium diets, but those restricted to 500- or 250-mg. low-sodium diets should substitute low-sodium milk for regular milk.*

## Cupcakes

2 cups sifted cake flour (not self-rising)
2 teaspoons low-sodium baking powder
¼ cup unsalted butter, margarine, or shortening
1 cup sugar
1 egg
¾ cup milk
1 teaspoon vanilla

Preheat oven to 375° F. Sift flour with baking powder. Cream butter; gradually add sugar, beating until light and fluffy. Beat in the egg thoroughly. Add flour mixture alternately with milk, beating after each addition until smooth. Blend in vanilla. Pour into 24 medium-sized paper baking cups in muffin pans. Bake 20 minutes.

*Makes 2 dozen cupcakes.*

# Almond Cookies

**1 cup unsalted softened butter or margarine**
**½ cup sugar**
**2 egg yolks**
**2 tablespoons water**
**1½ teaspoons almond extract**
**2½ cups sifted flour**

Preheat oven to 400° F. Cream butter; gradually add sugar and beat together until light and fluffy. Thoroughly mix in egg yolks, water, almond extract, and flour. Force dough through a pastry tube or cookie press onto ungreased baking sheets, using any shapes desired. Bake until golden (about 7 to 12 minutes).

*Makes 7 dozen cookies.*

# Index to Recipes

## Salad Dressings and Sauces

## Breads

## Desserts